TEN YEARS AFTER:
A Reminder

PHILIP GIBBS

By SIR PHILIP GIBBS

THE RECKLESS LADY

LITTLE NOVELS OF NOWADAYS

HEIRS APPARENT

THE MIDDLE OF THE ROAD

THE STREET OF ADVENTURE

WOUNDED SOULS

PEOPLE OF DESTINY

THE SOUL OF THE WAR

THE BATTLES OF THE SOMME

THE STRUGGLE IN FLANDERS

THE WAY TO VICTORY, 2 *Vols.*

NOW IT CAN BE TOLD

MORE THAT MUST BE TOLD

TEN YEARS AFTER:
A Reminder

BY

PHILIP GIBBS

NEW YORK
GEORGE H. DORAN COMPANY

FOREWORD

Since the last words of this book were written the political temper of the nation has been tested by the General Election and has been revealed by the mighty majority of the Conservatives, the dismissal of the first Labour Government, and the all but mortal blow to the Liberal Party.

It would be a bad thing for the British people if that sweeping change were the sign of reaction to wooden-headed principles of autocratic rule and class legislation. It would be a worse thing for the world. But the new Conservative Government will have no support from the majority of those who voted for it if it interprets its power as a mandate for militarism, jingoism, or anti-democratic acts. The verdict of the ballot box was, certainly, not in favour of any black reaction, but in condemnation of certain foreign, revolutionary, and subversive influences with which the Labour Party were believed, fairly or unfairly, to be associated.

It is true that the Labour Ministers had de-

[v]

nounced Communism, and during their tenure of office had revealed in many ways a high quality of statesmanship and patriotism. But all this good work was spoilt in the minds of many people of liberal thought, anxious to be fair to Labour, by the uneasy suspicion that behind the Labour Party, and in it, there were sinister influences foreign in origin, anti-British in character, revolutionary in purpose. Up and down the country some of its supporters indulged in loose-lipped talk about Social revolution, preached a class war, paraded under the Red Flag. Political incidents not quite clear in their origin, not fully explained, intensified this national uneasiness, developed into something like a scare, in minds not naturally hostile to Labour ideas. They made allowance for exaggeration, political lies and slanders, but when all allowance had been made, suspicion remained that if "Labour" were given a new lease of power it might play into the hands of a crowd fooling with the idea of revolution, not as honest as some of the Labour Ministers, not as moderate as the first Labour Government. It was a risk which the people of Great Britain refused to take. Mr. Ramsay Mac-Donald and his colleagues failed to prove their in-

[vi]

FOREWORD

dependence from their own extremists, and Liberal opinion entered into temporary alliance with Conservative thought to turn them out.

To men like myself, standing politically in "The Middle of the Road" between the extremists, the downfall of the historic Liberal Party is a tragedy and a menace. It brings the possibility of class conflict nearer by the elimination of a central balancing party of moderate opinion. That possibility will become a certainty if Mr. Baldwin's big majority drifts into reaction or into lazy disregard of urgent national distress. But I am inclined to believe that the new Government will be more Liberal than is pleasing to some of its reactionary supporters as Mr. MacDonald's Government was more moderate than the wild crowd who tried to force the pace. The nation as a whole will not tolerate black reaction any more than red revolution, and England stands steady to its old traditions of caution and common sense. Those qualities will be needed in times of trouble not far ahead.

PHILIP GIBBS.

CONTENTS

CONTENTS

[x]

CONTENTS

[xi]

PART I: THE WORLD WAR

TEN YEARS AFTER:
A Reminder

PART I: THE WORLD WAR

TEN years ago, as I write these words, a spiritual tremor, as though the last trump were sounding for the judgment of God, shook the souls of many peoples. Something incredible, inconceivable, frightful, was about to happen in a world which believed it could not happen. It was the beginning of the World War in which the most civilised nations on earth, as they believed themselves to be, were to be hurled against each other, with all their power, science, manhood, wealth, in a struggle to the death.

Ten years ago. . . . Not much in historical time, not a great span in the life of an individual, but so long, because of what has happened, that only by an immense effort of imagination can one's mind leap the gap between that time and this. One has to think back to another world in order to see

[13]

again that year 1914 before the drums of war began to beat. It is a different world now, greatly changed, in the mental outlook of men and women, in the frontiers of the soul as well as the frontiers of nations. Dynasties have fallen, kings are in exile, the political maps have been re-drawn, new nations have come into being, old nations have lost their pride and their place. And yet that is nothing to what has happened in the minds of men and women. Old habits of thought have been smashed; old securities, traditions, obediences, convictions, lie in wreckage and, unlike the ruins of the war itself, will never be restored. We are different men and women.

Ten years after! How brief a time since that August in 1914! A mere tick of the clock in the history of mankind, yet we who are alive after so much death, who were stirred by the first shock of that war, and lived through its enormous drama, can hardly get back to ourselves as we were before the War began. Were we indeed those men and women who thought, acted and agonised in those days? Did we really believe the things that were then believed? Were we shaken by those passions, uplifted by those emotions? Are we the people

[14]

who suffered and served? It is hardly possible to recapture, even in a dream, even for a few moments of illusion, the state of mind which was ours before the War happened and in the beginning of its history. It is very difficult because something has broken in us since then, and the problems of life have a different basis of thought, and all that emotion lies dead within us.

THE SENSE OF PEACE

In Europe, before it happened, there was a sense of peace in the minds of the peoples. Do they remember how safe they felt? French peasants in their fields were looking forward to a good harvest, the French shopkeeper to a good season. Alsace Lorraine? . . . An old sore, almost healed. Not worth re-opening at the price of the blood of a single French soldier! The German folk were drinking their laager beer as usual after days of industry. Their trade was good, they were capturing the markets of the world. Life was good. The Junkers and the militarists were talking rather loudly, and there was a lot of argument about Germany being "hemmed in" and "insulted" by

England, but it was, after all, no more than high-sounding talk. The German Army was supreme in Europe, unchallenged and unchallengeable. The German Fleet was the Kaiser's hobby. Who would attack them? Not France. Russia? Well, in East Prussia that was a secret fear, something like a nightmare, a bogey in the background of the mind—but really unthinkable. England? Bah! England was friendly in the mass and without an army worth mentioning. Poor old England! Weak and decadent as an Empire, without the power to hold what she had grabbed. One day per-haps . . . but not with Socialism spreading in Germany like an epidemic. Anyhow the good old German God was presiding over the destiny of the great German people, who were safe, strong, in-dustrious, prosperous, and, for the present, satis-fied.

In England this sense of peace, I remember, was strongest. It was hardly ruffled by any anxieties among the mass of our folk. There was trouble in Ireland. There always had been. The suffra-gettes were a horrible nuisance. Strikes were fre-quent and annoying. But the old order of English life went on, placid, comfortable, with a sense of

[16]

absolute security. The aristocracy grumbled at the
advance of democracy, but within their old houses,
their parklands and walled gardens, they were un-
disturbed. They had great reserves of wealth. The
beauty of the life they had built around them was
not invaded. Their traditions of service, loyalties,
sports, continued and would continue, they believed,
because those things belonged to the blood and spirit
of England.

Middle-class England was prosperous and con-
tented. Business was good in "a nation of shopkeepers," in spite of fierce competition. Life—
apart from private tragedy—was comfortable, gay,
with many social pleasures unknown in Victorian
days, with a greater sense of liberty in thought and
manners, and a higher standard of life for small
folk. "God's in His Heaven, all's right with
the world!"—barring politics, newspaper scares,
women's claims to votes—and Ireland. The people
of the British Isles felt utterly secure.

It was an inherited sense, a national tradition,
an unquestioned faith. It was their island pre-
rogative. Now and again wars happened, but they
only gave a touch of Romance to life. The sons
of the old families went out and died like gentle-

men, or came back to the music of brass bands, after
the usual victories over savage tribes, splendidly
described by artists and correspondents in the illus-
trated papers. Some of the young lads from factories and fields went off and took the King's Shil-
ling, and came back bronzed, with straighter backs,
and a few medals. The little Regular Army was
the best in the world for its size. Not even the Boer
War, with its blunders, its inefficient generalship,
and its drain upon youth and money, touched in any
vital way the foundations of English life, its reserves of wealth, or its utter faith in national security. The British Navy was supreme at sea.

The British people had no quarrel with any great
Power. All talk about a German menace, we
thought, was the delusion of foolish old gentlemen
in military clubs, or the scaremongering of newspapers out for circulation and sensation. The heart
of England beat steadily to the old rhythm of life
in country houses and fields and workshops and
mean streets. Beneath the surface of modern
change, progress and accidental novelties, the spirit
of England and of its sister peoples was deep-
rooted in the past and slow-moving towards new
ideas. Outside the big cities it was still feudal in

[18]

respect for the old "quality," the old distinctions of class and service. The English people felt themselves divided by a whole world from the Continent of Europe because of that strip of sea about them. They had nothing to do, they believed, with Continental quarrels, hatreds, fears, or armies. They were safe from invasion, and masters of their own destiny. The Empire was very useful for trade, peaceful in purpose, and easily controlled by a few regiments if troubles arose among Indian hillsmen or African tribes. They had peace in their hearts, no envy of other nations, no military ambitions.

The English-speaking peoples, including the United States, believed that the world was settling down to a long era of peace. War was abominably old-fashioned! It was out of keeping with modern civilisation and with its increasing humanity, decency, respect for life, lack of cruelty, and general comfort. The world had reached a higher stage of human brotherhood. Had not science itself made war impossible between civilised peoples? The financial interests of nations were too closely interwoven. Literature, art, education, good manners, and liberal ideas had killed the very thought of war. We had got beyond the Dark Ages. . . .

[19]

So England and America thought, or among those who did not think, felt—without question or misgiving.

Then the War happened.

THE CALL TO ARMS

Among the common folk—and I write of them—nobody knew at first how it happened, or why. An Austrian Archduke had been murdered at some place with a queer, outlandish name. Very shocking, no doubt; but what had that to do with John Smith watering his flowers in a suburban garden, or with Mrs. Smith putting the baby to bed? Still less with John K. Smithson, of Main Street, U.S.A., winding up his "flivver." Servia—where was Servia?—was threatened with an ultimatum by Austria. Those foreign politics! Russia was taking the matter up. What had it got to do with Russia? Kings and Emperors were exchanging telegrams; Germany was intervening, backing up Austria. France was getting excited. Why? What was it all about? Why did all that stuff, columns and columns in the newspapers, turn out the sporting news? It was all very dull and incom-

prehensible. Russia was "mobilising," it seemed.
Germany was threatening war with Russia, France
with Germany. Why? In Heaven's name, why?
What did it all mean? In the House of Commons
there were strange speeches; in the newspapers
terrible warnings, that England, too, might be
drawn into this conflict of nations. Preposterous!
The Cabinet was sitting late, hour after hour. Sir
Edward Grey—a noble soul—was working for
peace, desperately. There was still a hope. Surely
the world had not gone mad! Surely even now the
incredible could not happen. Germany could not
do this thing. The German people, good-hearted,
orderly, highly civilised, in some sense our kinsfolk;
surely to God they were not going to plunge the
world into ruin for the sake of an Austrian Archduke! In any case it was nothing to do with England—nothing at all—until every heart stood still
for a second at dreadful news.

Germany had declared war on Russia and France
was threatened. German troops were moving
towards the French frontier and towards the Belgian frontier. Germany was demanding a right of
way through Belgium to strike at the heart of
France. If the demand were resisted, she threat-

ened to smash her way through. Through Belgium, a little, neutral country, at peace with all the world, incapable of self-defence, guaranteed by Great Britain and Germany, by a treaty that the German Ambassador in London desired to treat as a "scrap of paper." God in heaven! If that were so, then there was no law in the world, no honour among nations, no safety for civilised peoples desiring peace. How could England, with any honour, stand by and see the fields of Belgium trampled under the feet of an invading army? With any shred of honour or self-respect? This was more than a threat against Belgium. It was a slash in the face of civilisation itself, a brutal attack upon all that code of law and decency by which we had struggled out of barbarism. So the leading articles said, and there was no denial in the heart of the people, though at first they had no thrill of passion but only a stupefaction in their minds. So Great Britain was going into this war? For honour's sake and the safety of civilisation? That would mean—who could tell what it meant? Who knew anything about modern warfare between the Great Powers with all those armies and navies and piled-up armaments? It would mean Hell, anyway.

[22]

THE WORLD WAR

On August 4 the British Government declared war on Germany for the violation of Belgian territory. On the following day at the mouth of the Thames the cruiser *Amphion* sank a German mine-layer, and so opened the first hostilities between the German and the British nations since their history began.

England was "in"—all in, with all her wealth, all her manhood, all her strength, to whatever the end might be, in a struggle for life or death, in which civilisation itself was at stake.

THE IGNORANCE OF THE PEOPLES

The peoples of Europe knew nothing of the forces which had led up to the conflict. They had never been told about the secret treaties—made by statesmen of the old school without their consent, though their lives were pledged in them—by which the Foreign Offices of Europe had played against each other for high stakes in a dangerous game called the Balance of Power. They were ignorant of the rivalries and greeds which had been inflamed for half a century by the rush for Africa, where France, Germany, Italy, Spain, and Great Britain had bargained and intrigued and quarrelled with each other for slices of the Dark Continent which had put a black spell upon the imagination of Imperialists in all these countries. They did not know that German Imperialists believed, not without reason, that England and France had squared each other in order to prevent German influence in Morocco, and that she felt herself thwarted by the two powers in all her ambitions for "a place in the sun," for the sources of raw material, and for the expansion of her trade. They were ignorant of Pan-German dreams of dominant power in Middle Europe, and of an Asiatic Empire following the line of Berlin to Bagdad. They were not aware of Pan-Slav ambitions cutting clean across Pan-German ambitions and looking forward to a future when the Russian Tsardom would have its second capital in Constantinople, and when the Russian race would stretch through Serbia to the Adriatic Sea. They had never realised the meaning of the Balkan Wars of 1912, when Russia was behind Serbia and Germany behind Turkey, in the first skirmish for these rival schemes. They were never told by their leaders that explosive forces were being stored up in Europe because of the rival Imperialisms which sooner or later were bound to result in infernal fire shattering the whole structure of European life.

All these things had been kept secret in the minds of kings and emperors, statesmen and diplomats, and the peoples in the mass went about their work without a thought of the dark destiny that was being woven for them in the looms of Fate. In Germany, it is true, the military caste, the Civil Service, and the Universities had been steeped in the poison of an Imperial philosophy based upon Brute Force and the right of the strong to seize the power and places of the weak. The Kaiser, picturing himself in "shining armour," with God as his ally, had made himself the figurehead of this school of thought. From time to time he uttered portentous words. He threatened with "a mailed fist" all who dared to cross the path of German aspirations. He vowed that he would "dash to pieces" all those who opposed his will. Even in Germany before the war these words were ridiculed by peace-loving citizens, scorned by millions of theoretical Socialists, and ignored by the peasants who were busy with their sowing and reaping in quiet fields. In England they seemed but the bombast of a theatrical

[25]

man born too late in the world's history for such mediæval clap-trap. Outside small circles, in touch with the undercurrents of international policy and afraid of unspeakable things, or ready to risk them, the common folk knew nothing of their peril, and were not allowed to know.

THE CALL TO COURAGE

Ten years ago! Who can remember the spirit of Europe then? Or his own mind? That sense of horror, chilling the heart of unimaginable things, that bewilderment because so monstrous a tragedy had come out of the blue sky, without warning, as it seemed, for trivial causes, and then—and then— a call to the secret courage of the soul, a dedication to service and sacrifice, a welling-up of old traditions, emotions, passions, primitive instincts, which had seemed dead and useless because of world peace and the security of civilisation.

In Great Britain it was as though the nation had been shaken by a great wind in which the Voice of God was heard. In those first days—and months—there was no degradation of the height to which the spirit of the British people was uplifted.

[26]

Even their enemies admit that. The petty, squalid, rotten things of life fell from them. They put away their own quarrels, self-interests, political and industrial conflicts. This thing was too big for those trivialities. It was bigger than individual lives, loves, hates, fortunes, homes or business. The old barriers of class, strongly entrenched in the structure of English life, were broken down with one careless and noble gesture. The sons of the great old families joined up with the shop boys, the peasants, the clerks, the slum-folk, and stood in the same ranks with them as volunteers in the "war for civilisation." The daughters of the county gentry, of the clergy, and professional classes went down on their knees with shop girls and servant girls, to scrub the floors of hospitals or do any kind of work. Those wild women who had fought the police for the Vote became ambulance drivers, nurses, farm girls, ammunition workers, needle women—anything for service. The rich poured out their money and the sons of the rich their blood. The poor offered their bodies and all they had. It took some time for England to understand this need of soldiers. It was not until after the Retreat from Mons and terrible despatches, revealing dreadfully that the little Regular Army was but a small outpost, half-destroyed after immortal valour against over-whelming odds in France, that the recruiting stations were stormed by the young manhood of the nation, from public schools, factories, city offices, and the little villages of the countryside. Husbands left their wives, lovers their sweethearts, fathers their children, scholars their books, and enrolled themselves, as they knew, for the chance of Death. And the women let them go, urged them to go, and hid their tears. There was not a mother in England at that time, or none that I knew or ever heard of, who, looking at the strained face of her son, held him back by any passionate plea when he raised his head and stared into her eyes and said: "I must go!"

The whole nation, apart from a few individuals, was inspired by a common loyalty to ideals which seemed very clear and bright. They believed, without any complications of thought and argument, without any secret doubts, that this war had come upon the world solely because of German brutality, unprovoked, against peaceful neighbours. Stories of German atrocity, some true and many false, in the first invasion of France and Belgium, deepened their horror for a nation which had threatened civi-

[28]

lisation itself with a return to barbarism, and under whose rule there would be no liberty, no life worth living. The chivalry of the British people, their love of fair play, their pity, were outraged by the trampling of Belgium and the agony of France, attacked by the greatest military power in the world. That was enough for them. That was what inspired them in their first rush to the rescue. It was only later that they understood the menace to their own Island and Empire, whose existence was at stake. In those early days, there was no self-interest in the spiritual uprising of England and her sister nations. There was a nobility of purpose, undimmed and untarnished, crystal clear to simple minds, knowing nothing and caring nothing for deeper causes of the war than German militarism and its brutal assault. Only the newspaper press vulgarised and degraded the splendour of this simple chivalry by its appeal to blood lust and its call to hate and many frantic lies.

THE HOMING BIRDS

From all parts of the Empire the old Mother Country saw her homing birds. From Canada,

[29]

Australia, New Zealand, South Africa, came bronzed and hardy men who were the uncles or the cousins or the brothers of the boys who were still storming the recruiting stations at home. After them came wave after wave of young manhood from the far Dominions, and for the first time in history the British Empire, so loosely linked, so scattered, so jealous of restraint or control from the British Government, was seen to be a federation of English-speaking peoples more strongly bound by links of sentiment and kinship in time of peril than any Imperialist of the old school could have forged by autocratic power. They were free peoples enlisting for service, as they believed also, in the cause of civilisation and in the chivalrous defence of peace-loving peoples wantonly attacked by a brutal enemy.

Looking back now with disgust of war and all its filthiness and death in our inmost souls, after years of disillusion with the results of that war, with a more complicated knowledge of its causes back in history; with a legacy of debt; unsettled problems; with new causes of hate, revenge, conflict; with justice no longer all on one side, nor injustice, one must still acknowledge the splendour

[30]

of that spiritual comradeship which made all classes offer themselves for service and sacrifice to the uttermost, which was death. Not in England, nor in France, nor later in the United States, was there any love of this war for war's sake. It did not appeal to the imagination of youth as a great adventure. Here and there its call might have come as a liberation from dull existence, or as an escape from private tragedy, or as a primitive blood lust. In very rare cases it appealed to old fighting instincts as a better thing than peace. To most it was hateful. Our young men loved life and loathed the thought of death. They did not want to kill or be killed. They disliked military discipline, dirt, lice, the thought of shell-fire, the foreboding of wounds, blindness, mutilation, and horror. They were the heirs of a civilisation in which there had been a high standard of decency, refinement, comfort, and individual liberty. Each young man when he went to the recruiting office knew in his heart that he was saying good-bye, perhaps for ever, to the things and folk he loved, to all familiar decent things, to the joy of life itself. Yet in millions they went, tide after tide . . . and the women hid their tears and their agony as best they could, and found work to do. In great houses and little homes there was the same spirit. Out of the foulest slums as well as out of fine houses came the heroic soul of a people proud of its history, impelled unconsciously by old loyalties which had been stunted but never killed by social injustice.

That was the passion of England and her sister peoples when war began. Difficult to imagine, impossible to feel again—now! . . . So much has happened since.

THE SPIRIT OF FRANCE

I remember the mobilisation in Paris on the day before war was declared, and that day. The French people had a different, sharper, more immediate fear. The frontier was in danger. France herself was menaced by the greatest army in the world. In one day, two days, all her life would be at stake. There was a sense of stupefaction among the common people. They too had been taken by surprise by the suddenness of the challenge. And they knew better than the English what war meant in horror and agony. In those crowds among whom I went there were many who remembered 1870—that

[32]

nightmare of terror and shame and tears. There
was no cheering, as when fifty years before the
people in Paris had shouted *à Berlin!* in an ecstasy
of war fever. In Paris there was the hush of souls
who looked into the face of great death. In the
streets men were parting from their women—for
the last time. Some wept, not many, after the
kiss of eternity. Emotion strangled one's heart.
In those days France seemed to me divine in courage, in sacrifice, in suffering. Anarchists, revolu-
tionists, the scum of the underworld, the poor drabs,
were cleansed of all evil, for a time, by love and
passion—for France. They themselves did not
matter. They held their lives as nothing so that
France might live. The Pacifists said: "This is a
war to end war." The Socialists said: "This is a
war against militarism." The old women said:
"Our sons will die, but France will be saved." The
young women said: "We give our lovers to
France." From the fields, the workshops and the
factories, the manhood of France, quicker than
in England, came down to the railways to join their
depôts, and for hundreds of miles on the first night
of war, in a train taking the first troops to the eastern frontier, I heard on the warm breeze the "Mar-

seillaise," the song of Liberty and France, and the
tramp of marching men, and the rattle of gun waggons; and I felt the spirit of an heroic people like
a physical vibration about me. After that come a
thousand memories, strangely distant now, like an
old dream, of roads black with fugitive people, re-
treating from the red flame of war; of French and
Belgian towns under the first shell-fire, until they
fell into flame and ruin; of wounded men, clotted
with mud and blood, very quiet, on dirty stretchers,
lying in rows under brown blankets, on railway
platforms, in improvised hospitals, piled in farm
carts, huddled under broken walls, in endless cara-
vans of ambulances; the reek of blood, disinfectants,
death; troops on the march, guns going forward,
the French cavalry riding on saddle-galled horses,
machine-guns in cornfields; troop trains; stations
crowded with regiments; fields strewn with dead;
women wheeling perambulators with babies and
household goods, boys pushing old men along in
wheelbarrows, farm carts laden with children, furniture, grandmothers; the cry reiterated of *"Sales
Boches!"*; the words *"C'est la guerre!"* repeated as
an endless reason for infinite resignation to all this
agony, and terror of civilian folk trapped in chaos;

[34]

the phantasmagoria of war in modern civilisation; and always the courage of women, the valour of men, the immortal spirit of France rising above the torture of its soul and body, while the enemy thrust closer to its heart. In those days—ten years ago—an Englishman in France dedicated his heart to these people. . . .

THE ENTENTE CORDIALE

And in those days the French people loved the English and their kinsfolk, so that when the first British troops appeared they went mad with joy, as I saw, kissing them, with streaming tears, dancing round them, flinging flowers to them, giving them fruit, as those boys, clean-shaven, bronzed, smart, laughing, singing, "It's a long, long way to Tipperary," went forward to be killed, wounded, maimed, blinded, broken, as most of them were before the end came, and some very soon. *Vivent les Anglais!* . . . Have the French people forgotten, or have we?

I was in Paris, after wild adventures, with two comrades on a day in September when it seemed that the city was doomed. It was already deserted.

[35]

At mid-day, between the Place de la Concorde and the Etoile, we saw only one man, and that a policeman on a bicycle. It was no longer the seat of Government. Vast numbers had fled. We had seen them storming the trains. All others sat indoors, with their shutters closed, waiting for the tramp of German soldiers down the streets. The German guns were as close as Chantilly. Only a miracle could save Paris, as we knew, having seen the retreat of a French Army through Amiens, and the stragglers of the British Army after the Retreat from Mons, and the advance of the enemy as far as Beauvais, and a hundred signs of impending tragedy. The sun was glittering on the golden eagles above one of the bridges. The palaces, domes, spires of Paris were clear-cut under a cloudless sky. All the beauty of the city, all its meaning to the world in knowledge and art and history, invaded our hearts. If Paris were taken and France beaten, civilisation itself would be defeated and life would be worthless, and God mocked. It could not happen like that. A miracle must happen first. For God's sake!

The miracle happened—the miracle of the Marne. The German tide was turned at last. By the blunder of the German Staff, by the audacity of Foch, by Galliéni with his army in taxi-cabs, by the desperate valour of French soldiers, fighting, dying, maddened by thirst, with untended wounds, with rage in their hearts, agonising, but without surrender in their souls because the life of France was in their guard that day. They won a victory which smashed back the German Army and destroyed their plan.

The British Army had a small share in that victory of the Marne. Its weight did not count for much, but its artillery harassed the German retreat with deadly execution, and in fighting down from Mons it had helped to spoil the German time-table and to bar the way to Paris for just that little time which enabled France to stand on its line of battle and repair the dreadful blunders of its first defence.

Have the French forgotten that? It happened ten years ago!

TRENCH WARFARE

The Germans were forced to dig in. It was the beginning of trench warfare. Then the line hardly altered for four years more, in spite of endless battles and unceasing death.

The British Regulars—that "contemptible little army" as the Kaiser called it before its rifle fire mowed down his men—were spent and done after the first and second Battles of Ypres, where they barred the way to Calais with a thin line standing among their dead. The Territorials—volunteers before the war—arrived, as steady as old soldiers. It was due to them that the Regulars had been able to get to France, leaving them for home defence. Then the new armies came into the field—"the Kitchener boys"—the First Hundred Thousand. They were those young men who had stormed the recruiting offices at the first call: from the Universities, public schools, city offices, village shops, and fields. They had been together in the ranks, learning each other's language, bullied by sergeant-majors, broken in by discipline, taught to forget the decencies of civilisation as they had known it in their homes, the little comforts of their former state, individual liberty. Already they had left their old civilian life far behind. Yet they came out to France and Flanders like schoolboys in keenness and enthusiasm. They wanted to get into the "real

[38]

thing" after all that gruelling training. They got into it quickly enough, up beyond Ypres at Hooge and St. Julien, or further south at "Plug Street" and Hill 60. They sat in water-logged trenches, with bits of dead bodies in the mud about them, under frightful shell-fire twenty times greater than the answer of their own guns because they were weak in artillery and short of shells. (The workers at home had not got into their stride in pouring out the engines of destruction.) They had no dug-outs worth the name. Only the Germans knew how to build them then, as they knew most else of war, as masters of technique, overwhelmingly superior in material, and in organisation. The British were in the low ground everywhere, with the Germans on the high ground, so that they could not march or move by daylight, or light a fire or cross a road, without being signalled to watchful eyes and shelled without mercy. They were lousy in every seam of their shirts. There was no chance of cleanliness unless they were far behind the lines. Young gentlemen of England—and of Scotland, Ireland and Wales—found themselves like cave men: eating, sleeping, living in filth and the stench of corruption, under winged death searching for their bodies. They saw their comrades blown to bits beside them; counted their own chances, coldly, made it one in four, with luck. They were afraid of fear. To lose control—that would be worst of all. To show funk before the other men, to feel themselves ducking, shrinking, weakening, under those cursed shrieking shells, to surrender will power— that would be fatal. Some did, gibbering with shell-shock, or shot as cowards; but few. The marvel was that youth could stand so much, and still make jokes, laughing at the frightful irony between their old life and this new one, between the old lessons learnt by nice little gentlemen in nurseries, and this bloody business and primæval stuff of killing and being killed!

It was truly a world war. Italy had come in. British troops were fighting in Africa and Asia. The Japanese Navy was in alliance with the British Fleet. Both France and England brought over coloured troops. Indian Princes poured out their wealth and offered their man power. Sikhs and Pathans rode through French fields. Gurkhas cut off the ears of German peasants after cutting their throats with curved knives. Indian cavalry, dismounted, were sent into the wet trenches of French

[40]

Flanders and died of cold if they did not die of wounds. Seneghalese negroes drove French lorries, were massacred as infantry. Moroccans were billeted in French villages and Arab chiefs rode through Dunkirk. Chinese coolies unloaded British shells and cut down French forests for British trench props. And the coloured races of the world were shown the picture of the white races destroying each other for some reason which was never clear to them. . . .

THE SLAUGHTER ON THE SOMME

The British Armies in France and Flanders reached their full strength before their great offensive on the Somme in the summer of 1915. In material and in manhood they were the best that England and the Empire could produce. The men were the fine flower of their race, in intelligence, physique, training, and spirit. In time of peace they would have lived to be leaders, administrators, artists, poets, sportsmen, craftsmen, the "quality" of their nation; the fathers of splendid children. They were in living splendour the priceless treasure of the British folk—and they were squandered,

[41]

wasted, and destroyed. . . . Behind them now was an immense power in artillery and ammunition and the material of destruction. The factories in England had been working at full pressure, millions of women had been stuffing shells with high explosives; guns, guns, guns came pouring up the roads towards the front in an endless tide; the ground was piled with ammunition dumps, and British Generals had at their command a fighting machine incomparable at that time, not only in weight of metal, but above all in freshness of enthusiasm and heroic human fire.

The British Armies rose out of their ditches for the great attack with an ardour that had never been seen before in the history of war, and in my judgment will never be seen again. They believed that at last—after artillery duels deciding nothing, after muddled battles like that of Loos, mining and counter-mining, and trench raids, and the gain of little salients at murderous cost—they were going to "do the trick" and end the war by irresistible attack. I saw the glory of those young men and the massacre of their bodies and hopes.

At the first assault after the greatest bombardment ever seen yet still leaving forests of barbed

[42]

wire and a fortress system of trenches and tunnels twenty miles deep behind the German front lines, they were mown down in swathes by German machine-gun fire, and afterwards, in isolated positions to which they staggered, blown to bits by German gun fire. By desperate courage they smashed through the outer earthworks of that infernal trench-system; for five months they fought through that twenty miles, yard by yard; but it was sheer slaughter all the way, and they were the victims of atrocious staff work, incompetent generalship, ruthless disregard of human life, repeated and dreadful blundering. The British Generals cannot be blamed. They were amateurs doing their best in an unknown type of war. They had to learn by failures and by mistakes. Perhaps their mistakes were not worse than those of the enemy's High Command; or not much worse. But for the men it was Hell. They were ordered to attack isolated positions, which often they captured although the whole arc of German gun fire for forty miles around was switched on to their bodies until they were annihilated. High Wood, Delville Wood, Trones Wood, Mametz Wood—a hundred more— are names that bleed with the memory of enormous

[43]

sacrifice of British youth. In the end they won through to open ground and forced the enemy into a far retreat to the shelter of the Hindenburg line.

The German losses in these battles of the Somme were frightful too, and for a time certainly broke the spirit of the German Army, as thousands of letters left in their dugouts proved beyond doubt. Their agony was as great as that of the British troops. They were pounded to death in their trenches and dug-outs, until all that land stank of their bodies, and one could not walk without treading on them. They were stunned by shell fire, tortured by fear beyond human control as they crawled out of their broken ditches to meet British bayonets. Their heroism was wonderful, as all our men confessed with an admiration which extinguished hate among those—nearly all—who had a sense of chivalry. But their losses, though enormous, were not as great as the British suffered, not half as great, I think, because defence was less costly than attack in those conditions. By the end of the battle of the Somme half a million of the finest manhood of Great Britain had been killed, wounded, blinded, shell-shocked, and broken.

[44]

The tide of wounded flowed back from the fields of the Somme in endless columns of ambulances, where the bad cases lay under brown blankets with only the soles of their boots visible. To the end of my life I shall remember those upturned soles and the huddled bodies above. The walking wounded formed up in queues outside the dressing stations: silent, patient, dog-weary, caked with a whitish clay. The casualty clearing stations were crammed, and the surgeons were overworked while, row upon row, the badly wounded were laid on the grass outside the tents or on blood-stained stretchers waiting for their turn. The "butcher's shop" in Corbie had a great clientèle. Whiffs of chloroform reeked across the roadways. Fresh graves were dug in cemeteries behind the lines, in spreading areas. The lightly wounded, after a little rest, came back laughing, cheering and joking. A Blighty wound! . . . Home again! . . . Out of it for a few months of grace!

THE SPIRIT OF THE VICTIMS

By the end of the Battle of the Somme the first impulses of the war had died down, the first emotions had been forgotten. Disillusion, dreadful experience, bitterness, had turned the edge of idealism. One cannot understand the mind of men ten years after without going back to that period of disenchantment. The young men who had hurried to the recruiting stations were on fire with enthusiasm for France and Belgium, for the rescue of liberty and civilisation, and for love of England. They became rather damped in the training camps because of so much red-tape, eyewash, spit and polish, and humiliation. They were handled, not like men filled with heroic spirit, but often like swine. Sergeant-majors swore at them in filthy language; old officers, too feeble for the front or sent back in disgrace for their incompetence, set them to ridiculous, time-wasting work. Reviews, inspections, parades, took the heart out of them. They had not joined for this . . . they were trained and staled by the time they went to France, though their spirits rose at the thought of getting into "the real thing" at last. They didn't like it. They hated it when its routine became familiar and horrible and deadly. They were ready to stick it out to the death—they did so—but certain values altered as their illusions

were shattered. It was all very well—though not
at all pleasant—to die for civilisation or liberty, but
it was another thing to die for some old General
they had never seen because he ordered them to
attack positions which were wrongly marked on his
maps, or because he was competing in "raids" with
the General commanding the line on his left, or because he believed in keeping up the "fighting spirit"
of his troops by ordering the capture of German
trenches which made another salient in his line and
were bound to be blotted out in mud and blood as
soon as the German guns received their signals.
Dulce et decorum est pro patria mori. Sweet to die
for one's country—in the first flash of enthusiasm—
and afterwards necessary anyhow, though distinctly
unpleasant to have both legs blown off, or both eyes
blinded, or one's entrails torn out. But not in any
way comforting to be sent over the top with a battalion unsupported on the right or left, or with
wrong orders, or without a barrage to smash the
enemy's wire, or by some incredible blunder which
meant the massacre of a man's best pals and a hole
in his stomach. Inevitable, perhaps. Yes, but un-
forgivable by its victims when it became a habit.
. . . Over and over again battalions were wiped out

because some one had blundered. It was the same on the German front, the French front, every front. And its effect on the minds of the fighting men was the same in all nations and on both sides of the line. It made them rage against the Staff. It made them feel that the front line men were being sacrificed, wasted and murdered by pompous old gentlemen and elegant young pups living very comfortably behind the lines in pleasant châteaux of France, far from shell fire, growing "flower borders" on their breasts. Men talked like that, with increasing irony. They were unfair, often. It's not easy to be fair when one's certain death is being ordered by influential folk who do not share the risks.

THE PEOPLE AT HOME

For England's sake! Yes, those young officers and men who went through the battles of the Somme and many others, seeing no end to the war, and the only chance of life in a lucky wound, endured everything of fear and filth, because at the back of their minds and hidden in their hearts was the remembrance of some home or plot of earth, some old village with an old church, which meant to them

—England, or Scotland, or Wales. They "stuck
it" all because in their spirit, consciously or unconsciously, was the love of their country, and in their
blood the old urge of its pride. But as the war
went on even this, though it was never lost and
flamed up again in the darkest hours, was overcast
by doubts and angers and ironies. They were all
so damned cheerful in little old England! They
took the losses of men as a matter of course. Business as usual and keep the home fires burning!
That was all very well, but those "charity bazaars
for the poor dear wounded," all that jazz and dancing and lovemaking, giving the boys a good time
in their seven days' leave, earning wonderful wages
in the munition works, making enormous profits out
of shipping and contracts, spending their money
like water, filling the theatres, keeping up the spirit
of the nation, wasn't it too much of a good thing
when viewed from the angle of a trench with one's
pals' dead bodies in No Man's Land, and a blasted
world around one, and death screaming overhead?

The profiteers were determined to "see this thing
through," to the bitter end. The Statesmen would
fight to the last man. The old gentlemen on military service boards were outraged by poor devils

with wives and babes who tried to evade conscription. At dinner parties and banquets these same old gentlemen, in clean linen, grew purple in the face with eloquence about the unthinkable shame of peace without victory. They would sacrifice their last son, or at least all their numerous nephews, on the altar of patriotism. They would go without sugar to the end of time rather than yield to a brutal enemy. Noble sentiments! But some of the sons and the numerous nephews who were going to be sacrificed on the altar of patriotism were secretly hoping that diplomacy, or strategy, or some miracle of God might find some decent way of peace before that sacrifice was accomplished. They were in love with life, those boys of ours. They didn't want to die, strange as it may have seemed to those who thought it was their duty to die and look pleasant about it.

They were unfair, those fellows who sat in wet trenches cursing the levity of England, writing sonnets, some of them about the murderous old men and the laughing ladies. It was true that some old men were making money—piles of it—out of all this business of war. It was true that some of the pretty ladies seemed callous of the death of the

[50]

boys they "vamped." It was true that large numbers of men in factories and workshops were making fantastic wages in safe jobs while poor old Tommy was dodging death in the mud for fourteen pence a day. It was true that war and casualties had become so familiar to the mind that many folk at home were beginning to accept it all as a normal thing. It was true that cheerfulness, gaiety, high spirits, were adopted as the only code of life, and that melancholy, fear, pessimism, prophets of woe, were barred as people of bad form. It was true that the imagination of the average man and woman at home was incapable of visualising a front line trench or a battlefield under a German barrage fire. It was true that the newspapers were full of false optimism and false victories. It was true that in a war against militarism England had been militarised, and that officers on seven days' leave from Hell-on-Earth were insulted by little squirts called A.P.M.'s because they didn't carry gloves or because their collars were too light in colour, with a thousand other tyrannies. It was true that the hatred of women against "the Huns" was not shared by men who had come to have a fellow feeling in their hearts for German peasants caught in the trap of war against their will, with no less courage than the men who killed them or whom they killed. It was true that parsons professing Christianity were more bloodthirsty than soldiers who cried out to God in hours of agony and blasphemed in hours of rage. It was true that in England in war time there was a noisy cheerfulness that seemed like callousness to those condemned to death. But it was *not* true that England was indifferent to the sufferings of the men, or that all that optimism was due to carelessness, or that all the laughing ladies were having the time of their lives because of war's delightful thrill and the chance of three husbands, or more lovers, in rapid sequence as battle followed battle and wiped out young life.

THE AGONY OF ENGLAND

Beneath the mask of cheeriness England agonised. Fathers grew old and white and withered because of their sons' sacrifice, but kept a stiff upper lip when the telegraph boy was the messenger of death. The mothers of boys out there suffered martyrdom in wakeful nights, in dreadful dreams, though they kept smiling when the boys came home between the battles and—worst of all—went back again. They hid their tears, steeled their hearts to courage. Even the pretty ladies—the most frivolous, the most light-hearted—gave their love so easily because it was all they had to give, and they would grudge nothing to the boys. Apart from a vicious little set, the women were beyond words wonderful in service and self-sacrifice. In spite of all the weakness of human nature and the low passions stirred up by the war, the British people as a whole during these years of great ordeal were sublime in resignation and spiritual courage. In millions of little houses in mean streets, and in all the houses of the rich, to which a double knock came with news of a dead or wounded boy, the awful meaning of the war burnt its way into the soul of the people. But they would not yield to weakness and had a stubborn obstinacy of faith in final victory—somehow, in a way they could not see. Anyhow, they wouldn't "let down" their men or show the white feather. They did not know that many of the men were sullen because of this unreasonable optimism, this "bloody cheerfulness." They did not know that in the trenches, under an awful gun fire, many men looked back to England as to an-

other world, which they no longer knew, from which
they were cut off by spiritual distances no longer to
be bridged, and for whose safety, frivolity, profiteers and prostitutes they were asked to die, to be
shell-shocked, gassed or mutilated, under incompetent generalship and for inadequate reasons.

The meaning of the war in those men's minds had
become less simple and clear-cut since the days
when it seemed a straight fight between idealism
and brutality—the Allies with all the right on their
side against the Germans with all the wrong. To
the end some men thought like that, and they were
lucky. They were the generals, the statesmen, and,
now and then, the fighting men with unbending will
and purpose. But to many of our officers and men
sitting in their ditches, as I know, the war was no
longer as simple as that. It was no longer, they
thought, a conflict between idealism and brutality.
It had developed into a monstrous horror, a crime
against humanity itself, in which all the fighting
nations were involved equally in a struggle for existence against powers beyond their own control.
The machinery of destruction was greater than the
men who were its victims. Human flesh and spirit
were of no avail against long-range guns and high

explosives. The common German soldiers, blown
to bits by our guns, torn to fragments by our mines,
poisoned by our gas, as our men were so destroyed,
had no more responsibility for these devilish things
than we had. It may have been so in the beginning
—though that was doubtful. What did they know
in their peasant skulls? But now they were just
the victims of the ghastly madness that had stricken
us all, of the crime against civilisation into which
we had all staggered. There was no getting out of
it, of course. The Germans had to be killed or they
would kill us, but the whole damned thing had happened against the will of those who on both sides
of the lines cowered under screeching shells and
hated it. Surely to God, they argued, it ought
not to have happened! It was civilisation that had
been at fault, not those poor devils in the mud and
mire.

It was the statesmen and politicians who were
guilty of this thing, or the Kings and the Emperors,
or the schoolmasters and the journalists, or the
whole structure of society based on competition
and commercial greed, supported by armies and
fleets, or the incurable stupidity of the human race,
or a denial of God in the hearts of men; but not

the fault, certainly, of those fellows from Bavaria and Saxony who were waiting for our next attack and writing picture postcards in their dugouts to women who would soon be widows. So many of our men began to talk and think, as every padre knows and as I know. So, even in France, the soldiers argued, if we may believe Barbusse and others, whom I believe as evidence of that. So certainly the German troops were thinking, as I heard from prisoners and afterwards from those who had fought to the last. The original meaning of the war altered, or was overwhelmed, as man sank more deeply into the mud and misery of it on both sides. It was only a few who held fast to its first principles of right and wrong, simple, clear, and utterly divided by a line of trenches and barbed wire.

UNBROKEN LOYALTIES

The "Long, long way to Tipperary" had carried our men far from the first enthusiasm with which they had joined up as "crusaders for civilisation." And yet they had an instinct of loyalty in them stronger than all their doubts, angers and ironies. Again and again, before their battles, and at the

[56]

worst time, it rose and carried them through to desperate endeavour or frightful endurance. It was loyalty to their own manhood, to their division and battalion, to their comrades, to the spirit of this hellish game, and to the old, old spirit of race which they could not deny. The orders might be wrong, but they obeyed. The attack might be doomed before it started—and often was—but they went over the top, all out. The battalion might be wiped out under high explosives, but the last of the living, lying among the dead, held on to their holes in the earth until they were relieved or killed or captured. Comradeship helped them. It was the best thing they had all through, and very wonderful; and, more wonderful still, they kept a sense of humour, whimsical, ironical, vulgar, blasphemous, and divine, which made them guffaw at any joke suggested by a pal and laugh in the face of death itself if it were not immediate in its menace. To the end the British Army kept that saving grace of humour, denied to the Germans, not so common with the French, but our most priceless gift in a world of horror. So they went on with the job of war, while the casualties tore gaps in their ranks.

New men came out to take their places. Fresh

contingents arrived from the Overseas Dominions.
There were new and monstrous battles. The Australians had already come to France after the tragic
epic of Gallipoli, in which they too had lost the
flower of their manhood. The Canadians had been
a strong link on the British front since the early
battles of Ypres. In England conscription took the
place of recruiting. There was to be no escape from
the ordeal for any able-bodied man unless he was
wanted for a home job or could get one to save his
skin or his conscience. . . . The war went on in
France and Flanders, in Italy, Russia, Palestine,
Turkey, Africa. The British Empire was all in,
everywhere, on sea and land. The area of destruction was widened as the months passed and the
years. Battles became more murderous because
the technique of war was becoming more "efficient,"
its weapons more deadly. Guns increased in number and in range. Poison gas supplemented high
explosives. Aeroplanes increased in size, in power,
and speed of flight; in bomb-dropping activity.
Tanks arrived. The British battles in Flanders five
months long, after those of Arras and Vimy and
Messines, were more ghastly, more sacrificial, than
those of the Somme. They were fought in mud and

blood. Men were drowned in shell craters. Battalions were blotted out by machine-gun fire, high explosives and gas shells.

THE WAR OF EXHAUSTION

The Germans gave way slowly, after stubborn defence, from every yard of cratered earth. Their own roads were choked with the traffic of the wounded—an endless tide of human agony. Behind them there was a welter of death and wreckage. Their man power was giving out on the Western Front. The collapse of Russia, stricken by infernal losses—four million dead!—with the very machinery of its life broken down under the weight of war, in revolt against the corruption of its own state, enraged by treachery from within, and weakened by a spreading anarchy among men who declined any longer to be slaughtered like sheep, gave Germany her last and only chance of flinging fresh forces on to the Western front and smashing through to victory by a last prodigious effort.

France was exhausted, but not yet spent. Her youth also had been thrown into the furnace fires recklessly, without a chance, time and time again, from the very beginning. Some of her generals had blundered, quarrelled, intrigued, while the manhood of France was bleeding to death. Battalions of young boys—as at Souchez—had flung themselves against almost impregnable positions and had fallen like grass before the scythe. Her coloured troops had been slaughtered like poor dumb beasts in storms of fire. Grand offensives in Champagne had been broken after losses hidden from the French people, though leaking out. The defence of Verdun, saving France from surrender, had drained it of its most precious life's blood. There were periods when France almost despaired, when there seemed no hope at all of final victory, but only of gradual extermination, which would leave France anyhow with but women and cripples and blinded soldiers and old men, and politicians, and profiteers. At the back there were periods of mortal depression. At the front the spirit of the men was sullen. There was mutiny in many ranks. They refused to be launched into another of those "grand offensives" at the bidding of generals who wasted blood like water. The French Army ceased fighting, while the British struggled in Flanders, at the cost of 800,000 casualties in five months.

[60]

THE WORLD WAR

Then came the crash of the German offensive in
March of 1918: against the British line first. They
had 114 Divisions, many fresh from Russia, against
48 under British command, tired after Flanders,
and thinly scattered over a big front. It was the
last thrust of the German war machine, and marvellously organised, directed and fought. The German Army, in spite of many blunders in High Command, had shewn a dynamic energy, a driving force,
a relentless will, and a marvellous valour which was
wellnigh irresistible. The German soldiers were no
less brave than the British or French, no less wonderful in self-sacrifice, no less enduring in agony.
Their final effort, when they put in the last of their
man power, was a supreme achievement to which
we must render homage if we have any chivalry in
our souls, in spite of a loathing of war which now
makes all such retrospect a nauseous horror. The
German sergeants and machine gunners who carried out the new tactics of "infiltration" were great
soldiers and gallant men.

The thin British line—after that struggle in
Flanders and battles round Cambrai—was broken

[61]

by the sheer weight of that terrific impact, and the British troops fell back fighting until, out of whole divisions only a few hundreds were left standing, and there was but a ragged line of exhausted men between Amiens and the sea.

The heart of the English-speaking peoples—all of them now, for the United States was with us at this time—stopped beating for a while, or seemed to do, as the news of that German advance went over the wires of the world. After all the battles of the French and English, their struggles, their slaughter, their sacrifice, their endurance, it looked for a little while as though it had all been in vain, and that all was lost. That was not ten years ago. It was less than seven. Yet can we recall even those days, when we felt stone cold, with a sharp anxiety thrusting its knife into our brains as the Germans came across the fields of the Somme, retaking all that ground which had been fought for yard by yard —drew near to Amiens, turned on the French, smashed their line as the British line had been smashed, and drove down to the Marne as in the first month of the war? Truly it looked like defeat. How near we were to that was only known at the time, perhaps even now, to those of us who saw with our own eyes the wild and tragic chaos of our falling back, the exhaustion and weakness of the French and British troops who had fought down to their last few men in every battalion, and the old battle grounds in possession of the enemy. Frightful weeks; ghastly emotions; scenes to sear one's imagination for ever. Yet now—hardly remembered so strange and self-protective is the human mind!

Looking back on that time, trying to recapture its sensations and philosophy, I cannot remember any absolute despair in England and France. By all the rules of the game we had nearly lost—within a hair's breadth—yet we did not acknowledge that. There was no cry of surrender from either of the nations, which still had a fixed faith that ultimately we should win, somehow. There was something astounding in the stolidity of the British people on the edge of great disaster. To men at the front it seemed ignorance of the extremity of peril. But it was the spirit of the race steadying itself again to fresh ordeals, unyielding in pride; they could not be beaten, it was unthinkable. To hint it was a treachery. If more men were wanted the youngest brothers would follow their older brothers. So it happened. Three hundred thousand boys of eighteen, the last reserves of Great Britain, were shipped over to France to fill up the frightful gap. From the factories which had been pouring out the material of war, not only for the British Army but for all the Allies, all but the most indispensable men were enrolled. The physically unfit, soldiers many times wounded, old crocks, were sent out to the depôts in France.

AMERICA COMES IN

One new power was almost ready for active service on the side of the Allies. If France could only hold out long enough, this new and arduous weight would be bound to turn the scale at last against German man-power, drained down to its last reserves. The United States Army was pouring into France with great tides of men, magnificent in physique, keen in spirit, and unscarred as yet by the fires of the war. They were untrained, ignorant of lessons that could only be learnt by deadly experience, and their Generals were novices in the organisation and handling of vast masses of troops, as the British had been. They were bound to make ghastly mistakes. They would waste their men as ours had been wasted, by faulty staff work; but sheer weight of numbers and the spirit of brave men would in the long run be irresistible. Had we the time to wait for them? . . .

We had been waiting long for them—too long as some thought, not realising the diversity of racial views in that great country and knowing little of its historical character and meaning. Vast numbers of its people had come from Europe in the past—distant or recent—to escape—Europe. They had wanted to get away from the very hatreds and rivalries which had led to this monstrous conflict. They desired to live secure, in a civilisation where the common man might work in peace and liberty without being lagged to fight for some King's quarrel or the ambitions of diplomats, or the fever of racial passion. Great numbers of them could not understand what the European quarrel was about when all was said and done. Anyhow, it had nothing to do with them, in the Middle West and the West, though New York seemed to be worried. Many intelligent Americans, shocked to the soul by this breakdown of civilisation in Europe, believed sincerely that the best service they could render the world was to stand on one side, to act finally as arbitrators between the exhausted nations among whom neither side could win—it looked like that—and to lead the stricken peoples back to sanity and peace. German Americans had a natural sympathy with the old fatherland though dismayed by its ruthlessness. Irish Americans still disliked England too much because of bitter and traditional memories to weep tears over her sacrifice or to glow with pride at the splendour of her spirit. Czechs, Slavs, Swedes were utterly neutral. In any case, apart from all racial strains, the war in Europe was enormously distant to the souls of men on isolated farmsteads, or to the crowds in the main streets of little towns west of New York. They elected President Wilson to keep them out of the war, and that strange man, with his mingling of mysticism and practical politics, his moral eloquence, and his autocratic methods, his mental disgust at war and violence, and his belief that the spiritual destiny of the United States was not to be fulfilled in terms of military force, or by any entry into the quarrels of the Old World, made them resist for a long time the strain of almost intolerable pressures, such as the German U-boat war and the rising passion of

American opinion, in many classes not neutral, not indifferent to the cause of France and Great Britain, but tortured by shame, impatience, rage, because the Government of the United States refused to call its people to a crusade on the side of right and justice.

All the old stock in America, or nearly all, millions of people in little American homes who read English books, whose minds were soaked in English history, whose ancestors had sprung from English and Scottish soil, panted for their deliverance from a neutrality which was a fraud and a shame in their hearts. They were not neutral. They never had been. They were all for England. Millions of others—remembering Lafayette, and filled with a deep sentiment for France, an enormous admiration for French heroism—enraged against Germany for the ruin she had made in France—loathed the policy of President Wilson, which seemed to them cowardly, selfish and unworthy. The pressure on Wilson became stronger and more insistent. Germany helped them in every possible way by deliberate insult, by methods of sea warfare outside the traditional code of common humanity; by plots, incendiarism, and sabotage within the United States itself in order to check the supplies of stores and ammunition addressed to England and France. When war was finally declared by the United States in the spring of 1917, the American people, apart from small minorities, were no longer neutral or indifferent, and a tidal wave of enthusiasm for service swept over all barriers and oppositions from coast to coast. It rose higher and higher as the months passed; reaching to a spiritual exaltation, unlike any emotion that had ever possessed that nation before. It had different motives, different manifestations from those which possessed the peoples of Europe engaged in the war. The Americans were not conscious of self-interest. There was no sense of menace against them such as Great Britain had partly felt. There was nothing they desired to gain for themselves. It was a crusade on behalf of civilisation. It was also unconsciously a desire in the American mind to prove that in spite of all their material wealth, their comfort of life, their peace and security, they were ready to suffer, to make sacrifice, to spend their energy, and their dollars, to give their manhood and their courage for a spiritual ideal. The United States would prove to the world that it had a national soul. It would

[68]

prove to itself that all the different strains of race within its citizenship had been merged and moulded into a national unity, responsive to the call of patriotism, disciplined by a common code, obedient to the voice of the State speaking for the whole people.

The very suspicion that certain sections of American citizens might be cold to this enthusiasm, even disloyal to the State, made American patriotism more self-conscious, demonstrative, and vociferous than in European nations where it was taken for granted. There was a spreading intolerance of the mass mind because of the need of unity. A non-comformist to this enthusiasm was marked down as a traitor or a shirker. Every American citizen, man, woman and child, had to prove allegiance to the state at war by some kind of service and self-sacrifice, in work or dollars or both. Woe betide all pacifists, conscientious objectors, or indifferentists. American methods of work, business organisation, industrial energy, dollar "drives," were all diverted from peace to war. Financiers, industrial magnates, engineers, organisers, gave their service to the State and "speeded up" the war machine. The entire manhood of the nation was

[69]

mobilised, drilled, equipped with an utter disregard of cost, and with driving zeal. It was a terrific demonstration of force, physical, moral, emotional, set in motion by generous impulses and terrific in potentiality.

In France and Flanders I saw the arrival of the first American troops, and then the following tide of men, behind the lines of the fighting front. It seemed to me then, as it does now, a miracle of history. After three hundred years the New World had come to the rescue of the Old. They marched over fields like those of Agincourt and Crecy where our bowmen and pikemen had fought before America was on the map of the world. And yet those men of the United States Army, different in type from ours, belonging to a different civilisation, spoke the English tongue, and no difference of accent could break our sense of kinship with them. Even though they did not all spring from our stock and blood they were in some way heirs of our tradition, our code of law, our root ideas. We watched them pass behind the lines with a sense of comfort and a kind of wonderment. They were magnificent men, untouched as yet by the strain of war, marvellously fresh, like our first youth which was now

[70]

dead. Their numbers grew and grew. One came
across their camps everywhere, but one question was
like a sharp sword in one's brain: Had they come in
time? The Germans were on the Marne again.
Paris was being shelled. Marshal Foch had no reserves. In a few days, if the Germans made another thrust, Paris might be surrendered and the
spirit of France broken, and the British Army involved in general defeat. Such things were un-
uttered. They were thrust aside even from one's
own mind. But they kept one's brain on the rack.

THE COUNTER-ATTACK

Then Foch attacked. As rapidly as his line of
blue men had come up to strengthen the British
Front after the German break-through—I shall
never forget the ride of the French Cavalry, on
lean horses wet with sweat, and the hurried tide of
blue transport waggons driven by coal black
negroes, and the endless line of guns with dusty,
sullen gunners coming to support us when our men
had fought back for three frightful weeks—he withdrew them from our Front. They vanished like a
dream army. English and Scottish Divisions were

[71]

entrained for the French Front. Our own lines were thin and weak. Foch was taking the ultimate risks. American infantry and American Marines were put in at Château Thierry for their baptism of blood. French infantry, withdrawn from other parts of the line, left almost without defence, were rushed to the Marne. The German salient thrust out like a battering ram, pointing to Paris, was attacked on both sides, at its junctions with the main line. It was pierced and broken. The enemy was panic-stricken and thrown into a mad disorder.

"Who attacked?" asked German prisoners.

"Foch's Army of Reserve," was the answer.

"He has no Reserves!" they said with rage. "It was impossible for him to have an Army of Reserve."

It was an Army of Reserve gathered piecemeal, flung together, hurled forward in a master stroke of strategy, at the last minute of the eleventh hour. It was the second "Miracle" of the Marne.

That battle broke the spirit of the German people and of the German Army. They knew that only retreat and defeat lay ahead of them. They had struck their last great blow and it had failed. They had used up their man-power. They, certainly, had

[72]

no Army of Reserve. They could only hope that the French and British were as exhausted as themselves and that the Americans were still unready. They prepared for a general retreat when the British Army took the offensive of August of 1918 and never stopped fighting along the whole length of its line until the day of armistice, while the French and Americans pressed the Germans on their own front.

The American Army, inexperienced, raw, not well handled by some of its generals, fought with the valour which all the world expected, and suffered great losses and made its weight felt. The sight of the American troops was a message of doom to the Germans. They knew that behind this vanguard was a vast American Army, irresistible as a moving avalanche. However great the slaughter of these soldiers from the New World, pressing on in the face of machine-gun fire, and lashed to death, millions would follow on, and then more millions. The game was up for Germany, and they knew it, and were stricken. Yet they played the game, this grisly game, to the end, with a valour, a science and a discipline which was the supreme proof of their quality as great soldiers. It was a fighting retreat, orderly and controlled, although the British Army never gave them a day's respite, attacked and attacked, captured masses of prisoners, thousands of guns, and broke their line again and again.

THE LAST THREE MONTHS

That sweep forward of the British in the last three months was an astounding achievement. They were the same men who halted on the armistice line down from Mons as those who had begun the attack three months before. They had few reinforcements. They had gone beyond their heavy guns, almost out of reach of their transport. Their losses had been heavy. There was no battalion at more than half its strength. They had been strained to the last fibre of nervous energy. But they had never slackened up. They were inspired by more than mortal strength, by the exultation of advance, the liberation of great cities, the rescue of populations long under German rule, the fever of getting forward to the end at last.

The delirious welcome of the liberated peoples awakened some of the first emotions of war which had long seemed dead. The entry into Lille was unforgettable. The first men in khaki were surrounded by wild crowds of men and women weeping with joy at the sight of them. Their buttons and shoulder straps were torn off as souvenirs. They were kissed by old women, bearded men, young girls, babies. Once again rose the cry of *"Vivent les Anglais!"* as in the beginning of the war. Our men were glad to be alive that day to get the welcome of these people who had suffered mental torture and many tyrannies during those four years under German rule. The fire of gratitude warmed cold hearts, relit enthusiasm, made it all seem worth while after all. Surely the French in Lille, the Belgians in Bruges, the people of Tournai, Cambrai, Valenciennes, Liége, have not forgotten those days of liberation. Surely *they* did not join in the cynical chorus which rose against England in France, or at least in the French press, during the years that followed? That to me is unbelievable, with those memories in my heart.

It was Marshal Foch himself who acknowledged with generous warmth that in these last months of war it was the hammer strokes of the British Army which did most to break the German war machine to bits, by enormous captures of prisoners, guns, and ground. General Ludendorff has said so, squarely, in his books; and history will record it, though it was quickly forgotten in some countries and never known in others. It is only for the sake of truth that it is worth recalling now, for there is no boast of victory in the hearts of men, knowing its cost and its horror, and no glory left about that war except the memory of the world's youth which suffered on both sides of the line.

THE COMING OF PEACE

So it ended, with a kind of stupefaction in the minds of the soldiers. It was an enormous relief, followed by a kind of lassitude of body and spirit. Ended at last! Incredible! At the front on the day of armistice there was no wild exultation, except in a few messes here and there behind the lines. The men who had fought through it, or through enough of it to have been soaked in its dirt, were too tired to cheer or sing or shout because peace had come. Peace! What did that mean? Civilian life again? Impossible to readjust one's mind to that. Impossible to go home and pick up the old threads of life as though this Thing had not happened. They were different men. Their minds had been seared by dreadful experience. Now that peace had come after that long strain something snapped in them.

Many of them had a curiously dead feeling at first. They thought back to all the things they had seen and done and suffered, and remembered the old comrades who had fallen on the way. Perhaps they were the lucky ones, those who lay dead, especially those who had died before disillusion and spiritual revolt against this infernal business. A war for civilisation? . . . Civilisation had been outraged by its universal crime. A war against militarism? Militarism had been enthroned in England and France. Liberty, free speech, truth itself, had been smashed by military orders and discipline over the bodies and souls of men. A war against the "Huns"? Poor old Fritz! Poor bloody old Fritz! Not such a bad sort after all, man for man and mass for mass. They had put up a wonderful fight. The glory of victory? Well, it had left the world in a mess of ruin, and the best had died. What would come out of this victory? What reward for the men who had fought, or for any nation? The profiteers had done very well out of war. The Generals had

[77]

rows of ribbons on their breasts. Youth had perished; the finest and noblest. Civilisation had been saved? To Hell with a civilisation which had allowed this kind of thing! No, when peace came, there were millions of men who did not rejoice much, because they were sick and tired and all enthusiasm was dead within them. They were like convicts after long years of hard labour standing at the prison gates open to them with liberty and life beyond. What's the good of life to men whose spirit has been sapped, or of liberty to men deprived of it so long they were almost afraid of it? Strange, conflicting emotions, hardly to be analysed, tore at men's hearts on the night of armistice. Shipwrecked men do not cheer when the storm abates and the bodies of their dead comrades float behind them. Nor did our men along the front where it was very quiet that day after a bugle here and there sounded the "Cease fire!" and the guns were silenced at last. Peace! . . . Good God!

PART II: THE UNCERTAIN PEACE

PART II: THE UNCERTAIN PEACE

TEN years after. . . . The memory of the war days is fading from the mind of the world. The ten million dead lie in their graves, but life goes marching on. Self-preservation, vital interests, new and exciting problems, the human whirligig, are too absorbing for a continual hark-back to the thought of that mortality. We are no longer conscious of any gap in the ranks of youth, torn out by the machinery of destruction. We do not realise the loss of all that spirit, genius, activity and blood, except in private remembrance of some dead boy whose portrait in uniform stands on the mantel-shelf. A new generation of youth has grown up since the beginning of the war. Boys of ten at that time of history are now twenty; and not much interested in that old tale. Girls who were twelve are now mothers of babes. The war! Bother the war! Let's forget it and get on with life. In that youth is right. It is not in its nature nor in moral health to dwell on morbid memories. But it is hard on

[81]

those whose service is forgotten—so soon. In England—ten years after—there are still 58,000 wounded soldiers in the hospitals—and in France great numbers more; but they are hidden away, as a painful secret of things that happened. Only now and again the sight of their hospital blue in some quiet country lane, near their hiding places, shocks one with a sharp stab of remorse. We had forgotten all that. We hate to be reminded of it.

FADING MEMORIES

Even the men who fought through those years seldom speak of their experience. It is fading out of their own minds, though it seemed unforgettable. They are forgetting the names of the villages in France and Flanders where they were billeted, or where they fought, or where they passed a hundred times with their guns and transport under shell fire. Good heavens!—don't you remember?—that place where the waggons were "pasted," where the Sergeant-Major was blown to bits, where old Dick got his "Blighty" wound? No. Something has passed a sponge across those tablets of memory —things that happened afterwards. Now and

[82]

again at Divisional banquets officers try to revive
the spirit of those days and exchange yarns about
trench warfare and days of battle. It is queer
how they remember only the jokes, the laughable
things, the comradeship, the thrill. The horror has
passed.

Something else has passed; the comradeship itself,
between officers and men, between all classes united
for a time in common sacrifice and service, annihilating all differences of rank and social prejudice
and wealth at the beginning of the war. It seemed
then as though nothing could ever again build up
those barriers of caste. The muddiest, dirtiest, com-
monest soldier from the slums or the factories or
the fields was a hero before whom great ladies were
eager to kneel in devotion and love, to cut away his
bloodstained clothes, to dress his wounds. In the
canteens the pretty ladies slaved like drudges to
give cocoa or any comfort to "the boys" from the
front. In the trenches or in ruins under shell fire
young officers wrote home about their men:
"They're too splendid for words! . . . I am proud
to command such a topping crowd. . . . They
make me feel ashamed of things I used to think
about the working man. There is nothing too good

[83]

for them." The British Government thought so too, and promised them great rewards—"homes for heroes," good wages for good work, "a world safe for democracy."

THE BARRIERS OF CLASS

Ten years after, the classes have fallen apart again. The old hostilities between Capital and Labour have been revived with increasing bitterness in many minds. The old barriers have been rebuilt in many countries. For a time, even in England, there was a revolutionary spirit among the men who had served, and a sense of fear and hostility against those who had said that nothing was too good for them. "Our heroes" became very quickly "those damned socialists," or those "dirty dogs" who are never satisfied, or those lazy scoundrels who would rather live on the "dole" than take an honest job. The men who had saved England were suspected of plotting for her overthrow, subsidised by Russian money and seduced by the propaganda of a secret society inspired by the spirit of Anti-Christ.

Ten years after the closing up of ranks, the surrender of self-interest, and a spiritual union, England is again seething with strikes, industrial conflict, political passion, and class consciousness. There are still a million and a quarter unemployed officially registered in Great Britain, and half a million more not on the registers and worse off. Instead of "homes for heroes" the working people in the great cities are shamefully overcrowded. In the agricultural districts of England young men who fought in the Last Crusade and marched with Allenby to Jerusalem, or those boys who left their fields in '14 for the dirty ditches in Flanders—for England's sake—are getting twenty-five shillings a week, upon which a single man can hardly live and a married man must starve. And ten years after they poured out their blood and treasure without a grudge, without reservation, first in the field and last out of it, the old "quality" of England or their younger sons are selling up their old houses to pay taxes which are extinguishing them as a class, depriving them of their old power and prerogatives, and changing the social structure of the nation by an economic evolution which is almost accomplished. On both sides there is bitterness, a sense of injustice, and an utter disillusion with the results of victory.

[85]

TEN YEARS AFTER

Ten years after the beginning of the war there
is no sense of security in Europe or the world.
"The war to end war," as it was called, has done
nothing of the kind. Beneath the surface of the
present peace there is a lava of hatreds and re-
sentments which bode ill for the future peace of
the world. There are larger standing armies in
Europe now than in 1913. There are more causes
of quarrel, and none of the old quarrels have been
extinguished—those racial rivalries, those national
ambitions, that commercial competition. The war
settled no argument for more than a period of exhaustion. The idea of a "world safe for democracy"
is falsified ten years after by a swing-back to extreme forms of nationalism and autocratic government through the greater part of Europe excepting
the British Isles and France. The German Republic, established after annihilating defeat, is only
biding its time for the return of monarchy, and its
present government is anti-democratic. Parliamentary institutions, the safeguard of democracy,
have been overthrown or contemptuously treated in
many nations. Italy, Spain and Hungary are

[86]

under military dictatorships. Russia is governed by a new-fangled tyranny under which there is no liberty of speech, conscience or economic life. Turkey, powerful again, is ruled by a committee of generals. Poland, Czecho-Slovakia, Belgium, are in military alliance with France, which, under Poincaré, ridiculed the possibilities of peace based on the goodwill of its neighbours, and relied for safety on a supreme army and the rule of Force.

THE PEACE TREATY

The Treaty of Versailles, which imposed the terms of peace upon Germany and her Allies, after their complete surrender, was the direct cause of all the troubles that beset us after the war. It violated the hopes of all moderate minded people, who believed that the world, after its frightful lesson, was ready for a new chapter of civilisation in which militarism might be overthrown as the greatest curse of life, and in which the common folk of nations might be made secure in their homes and work by a code of international law and arbitration. The statesmen who presided over the Peace Conference—Clemenceau, Wilson, Lloyd

George—had the fate of the world in their hands. Waiting for their decisions, their new plan of Europe, was a world of emotionalised men and women, ready and eager then, for a little while, to respond to a generous idealism which would lift all peoples above the morass of hatred and misery into which they had fallen. The German and Austrian peoples, starved and defeated, without a rag of pride left to cover their humiliation, fierce with anger against their war lords—their Junkers and their politicians of the old brutal caste—were ready also, for a little while, to join hands with the world democracy in a new order of life. They were conscience-stricken, ready to make amends, resigned to an awful price of defeat—provided they were given their chance of recovery and the liberty of their national life. They clung desperately to the words of President Wilson who, before their surrender, had in his Fourteen Points and other messages to the world outlined a peace which would be generous to the defeated if they overthrew their old gods, and would be based on justice, the rights of peoples, and the commonwealth of nations rather than upon vengeance and hatred.

Fair words, holding out prodigious hopes of a

new and better world! But when the terms of the Peace Treaty were made known they struck a knock-out blow not only to German hopes but to all the ideals of people who had looked for something nobler and more righteous by which the peace of the world should be assured. It was a peace of vengeance. It reeked with injustice. It was incapable of fulfilment. It sowed a thousand seeds from which new wars might spring. It was as though the Devil, in a jester's cap-and-bells, had sat beside Clemenceau in his black gloves, and whispered madness into the ear of Wilson, and leered across the table at Lloyd George, and put his mockery into every clause. In that Hall of Mirrors at Versailles the ideals for which millions of men had fought and died—liberty, fair-play, a war to end war, justice—were mocked and outraged, not by men of evil, but by good men, not by foul design, but with loyalty to national interests. Something blinded them.

The Territorial clauses of the Treaty, based theoretically upon "the self-determination of peoples," created a dozen Alsace Lorraines when one had been a sore in Europe. The old Austrian Empire was broken to bits—that was inevitable—but Aus-

[89]

tria, with its great capital of Vienna, was cut off from its old source of life, condemned to enormous mortality—which happened—and many of its people were put under the rule of their ancient enemies. The Austrian Tyrol is now the Italian Tyrol. Austrian property and populations are now in the hands of Czechs and Slovaks and Serbians. Hungary was parcelled out without consideration of nationality or economic life. Lines were drawn across its waterways, its railway system and its roads. Its factories, forests and mines were taken from it. Many of its folk were handed over to Roumanians and other hostile peoples. The German colonies in Africa were divided between Great Britain, France and Belgium, although it is a biological necessity that Germany should have some outlet for the energy and expansion of her population if another war may be avoided. The Danzig corridor was made between one part of Germany and another. Greece was given an Empire in Asia Minor and Thrace, over Turkish populations which she could only hold by the power of the sword at the cost of a future war—which she has already fought and lost, abandoned by the Governments which yielded to her claims.

[90]

THE UNCERTAIN PEACE

The resurrection of Poland, by which one of the greatest crimes in history was blotted out, and the national liberty given to the peoples of Esthonia, Latvia and Lithuania, stand to the credit of the peacemakers, although these new nations have no security in the future if Europe relies upon force rather than law. Other frontiers drawn carelessly across the new map of Europe will be blotted out in blood if ever again the passions stirring from the Rhine to the Volga rise against the barriers imposed upon them in this uncertain peace.

THE FANTASTIC FIGURES

But it was on the economic side of the Treaty and in its interpretation that the statesmen of the Allies seemed to be stricken with insanity, which infected many of their peoples until recent months. Germany, they insisted, had to pay all the costs of the war, for the damage she had inflicted and the ruin she had caused. Theoretically, that was just if one took the view that every German peasant, every German mother in a cheap tenement, every German worker on starvation wages, every little sempstress, or University student, ten or twelve years old when

[91]

the war began, shares the responsibility of those war lords and militarists who challenged the world in 1914.

Practically it was not only unjust but idiotic, because it was impossible, as everybody now acknowledges. It is almost beyond the scope of mathematics to calculate the losses of the Allies in the war. The British Government spent more in four and a half years of war than in two and a half centuries previously. Could Germany pay that back? England advanced two thousand million sterling to her Allies, and borrowed nearly a thousand millions from the United States on behalf of her Allies. Could Germany pay all that? France had borrowed vast sums from her peasants and shopkeepers which she debited against Germany; she owed Great Britain nine hundred millions sterling, she had to restore the great track of ruin, with all its destroyed homes, churches; farmsteads, châteaux —thousands of villages wiped off the map so that hardly one stone remained upon another—at a price which has loaded her with increased burdens of debt far in excess of actual cost because French contractors desired enormous profits. It was right and just that Germany should repair that damage in the

[92]

war zone, every brick of it and every stone. But could she do so in money payments, in addition to all those other claims? Could she pay also for war damage in Belgium, in Poland, on the high seas, wherever her guns had reached? Italy had great claims against Austria. Could Austria, brought to the edge of ruin, amputated, lopped of all sources of wealth, pay that bill of costs? Could Germany, the chief debtor, pay for the British unemployed in the "devastated districts" of England and Scotland, whose ruined trade was due to the war? All that, and then the pensions of wounded soldiers and the widows of dead men and orphan children? It would have been splendid if that were so. It might have been just even to bleed the working folk of Germany, the younger generation, the old women, the wounded and cripples even, the victims and heirs of their war lords, to the last pfennig in their purses, if it is justice that the individuals in a nation and their children and children's children are responsible for the guilt of their Governments. But, justice or injustice apart, the absurdity, the wild impossibility, of extracting all that vast tribute from the defeated enemy in terms of transferable wealth, ought to have been manifest to the most ignorant schoolboy of thirteen or fourteen years of age. Yet it was the illusion passionately professed by many great statesmen, by sharp-witted business men, by bankers and financiers, and by the gullible public who took their word for it, in France, Great Britain, and the United States.

THE GOLDEN LIE

Or was it just one great lie to deceive the people of the victorious nations and to keep them quiet by golden promises which the liars knew in their hearts could never be fulfilled? One is tempted sometimes to think so. It is now so transparently clear that not even the richest and most powerful nation in the world of commerce—the United States of America—could pay one tenth of the sum expected from Germany after her overwhelming defeat, and the ruin of her world trade, without overwhelming financial disaster, that it is incredible that the greatest statesmen of the Allies and all their experts and advisers could ever have believed in such mad economics. Year after year there were assemblies of financial gentlemen who solemnly sat round tables estimating Germany's ca-

[94]

pacity to pay. Year after year they reduced their estimates until they were brought down to 6,600 millions, and then by easy stages to 2,200 millions, while Europe sank deeper into economic misery; while British trade declined; while Austria starved; while France grew desperate for these payments; while Russia was famine-stricken; while Germany poured out paper money which became worthless, until her bankruptcy could no longer be concealed.

Future historians will be baffled by that psychology. They will hunt desperately for some clue to the mystery of that amazing folly which took possession of many people. They will call it perhaps the Great Financial Hoax, and argue that it was a deliberate deception on the part of the world's leaders, afraid to confess to their nations that after all their sacrifice there would be no "fruits of victory," but only heavy taxation, to pay for the costs of war which could not be shifted on to enemy nations. I do not think it was quite as simple as all that. I think in the beginning that sheer ignorance of the most elementary economic laws led men like Clemenceau and Lloyd George to over-estimate the power of a nation like Germany to transfer wealth in money values to other nations. They did not un-

[95]

derstand that all transferable wealth—or nearly all —can only be obtained by a trade balance of exports and imports, and that the potential energy of a nation, its factories and plants, its public buildings, bridges, organisation and industry, are not transferable except by a balance over exchange of goods. They were so hopelessly ignorant of international finance that they actually did believe that they could "squeeze" Germany of vast sums of money which could be divided among the Allies for the settlement of their immense bill of costs, without damaging their own trade or allowing Germany to trade unduly in the markets of the world. One British statesman promised his people that Germany should be squeezed like an orange until the pips squeaked. French statesmen, like Poincaré, dazzled the eyes of their people with golden visions. They balanced their budget by the simple method of assuming that all that war debt would be paid by Germany when pressure was firmly applied.

It was only later, when the politicians began to get a clear notion of economic laws, by the painful lessons of reality and disillusion, that they began to deceive their peoples and keep up the bluff. They were afraid to tell the truth after all those falsities. In France, long before the entry into the Ruhr, French economists, business men and senators confessed privately that France could never hope to get anything like her claims against Germany, and some of them, more candid than others, shrugged their shoulders and said: "We dare not tell the people—the shock would be too great." The French Press kept up the conspiracy of this deception, audaciously and persistently throwing the blame of delay in getting German payments upon Great Britain who did not stand by them in exerting "pressure." In Great Britain, dependent upon export trade for her main source of wealth, and seeing the deadly stagnation of Europe and its increasing loss of purchasing power, the truth of economic law was more quickly perceived, and its statesmen shifted their policy and forgot their golden promises more rapidly and with more public candour.

THE DOWNFALL OF IDEALISM

Looking back upon the years after the war, one sees that the idealism, which for a little while might have changed the face of the world if there had been great and noble leadership, fell with a crash in many hearts because the interpreters of the Peace Treaty were appealing not to the highest but to the lowest instincts of humanity; to greed rather than justice; to vengeance rather than reconstruction; to lies rather than truth. If only there had been one great leader in the world who had cried: "We were all involved in this crime against humanity, although Germany's guilt was greatest; let us in the hour of victory put vengeance on one side and so shape the peace that the common folk of the world will have a better chance of life," I believe that in the time when the agony was great and the wounds were still bleeding the hearts of people would have leapt up to him. They would have responded if he had pleaded for generosity to the defeated nations, if he had refused to punish the innocent for the guilty, if he had asked them to forego the pound of flesh demanded in the name of Justice, to forget the horror of the past, to escape from it together, to march forward to a new chapter of civilisation not based on standing armies, balances of powers, and cutthroat rivalry, but upon new ideals of international law, business, common sense, and Christian ethics.

[98]

THE UNCERTAIN PEACE

People will say—do say—"It would have been weakness to let the Germans off. They deserved to be punished. They would have made a peace of terror, if they had had the chance of victory. There is Justice to be considered. Justice demands its due, or God is mocked."

That is all true. It would have been weakness to let the Germans off, but the surrender of their Fleet, the destruction of their Army, the enormous sum of their dead was not a "let off." They were broken and punished, in pride and in soul. They would have made a peace of terror! Yes, that is certain, and they would have aroused, intensified and perpetuated a world of hate by which later they would have been destroyed. Their war lords would have made a worse peace than this of ours, but that is no argument why we should have imitated their methods and morals.

THE LEAGUE OF NATIONS

There was one institution created by the peace-makers which held out a promise of a better relationship between nations than that of military alliances and armed force divided into an uncertain

Balance of Power. All that was wrong in the Peace Treaties might be put right by the League of Nations. The seeds of war sown by the Treaties might be made to blossom into the laurels of peace by the League. Although the Supreme Council set up by the Allies for the enforcement of its military provisions might act on purely nationalistic lines, the League of Nations would build up the international moral sense, and establish a Court of Appeal by which injustice, aggression, and the war spirit could be extirpated between all nations subscribing to its code of laws, and the spirit of arbitration.

President Wilson comforted himself for any little defects which might have crept into the Peace Treaties by this new instrument of idealism which he had helped to create with a very passionate enthusiasm. It was his great gift to the world and, as he hoped, the fulfilment of the promises he had made to the world in his messages before and after the ending of the war, appealing so poignantly to the secret hopes of humanity that when he came to Europe as the great arbitrator of its councils, he was received as the leader, spokesman, and prophet of the New World which was to be built out of the ruins of the Old. The rejection by the American Senate of all that he had done killed Wilson. It also destroyed all immediate hopes of European recovery based upon the League as an instrument of reconstruction, co-operation and peace. It was one of the great tragedies of history. Yet, looking back now upon the reasons of the American refusal to enter the League of Nations, it is clear that it was not entirely due to the personal antagonism which President Wilson had aroused by certain defects of character—his autocratic methods, his rejection of good counsel, and his mentality in the beginning of the war, nor to a national selfishness on the part of the American people, desiring to withdraw rapidly from responsibilities which they had incurred by their entry into the war. From the American point of view, at that time, the war had proved more than ever the supreme good fortune of the United States in being remote from the hatreds and quarrels of that mess of races in Europe out of which their people had escaped in the past. They did not understand Europe. They had no direct interest in its national rivalries. They could not control or abate its passions. All opponents of the Wilson policy regarded it as a calamity that

[101]

the United States should surrender its geographical immunity from the evil heritage of the Old World and deliberately involve its future in that arena of ancient feuds. By entering the League of Nations it seemed to many that the people of the United States would be dragged into new wars in which they would have no direct or indirect interest, and that they would have to support and enforce the maintenance of European frontiers, redrawn by the Peace Treaties, and already the cause of passionate resentment. They did not approve of all that parcelling up of territories which had taken place under the benignant name of "mandates"—British dominion in Palestine and Mesopotamia, French rule in Syria, the gobbling up of German Africa, the Greek Empire in Asia Minor. Were they to use their strength to support that new combination of powers which one day was bound to be challenged and resisted? Above all was the New World to enter into military alliance with France and Great Britain to support a policy of domination in Europe which could only last as long as the German people and their Allies were suffering from war exhaustion—a one-sided pact which would make for the tyranny of certain powers, or

[102]

at least their military supremacy, over other nations of the world? That would be a surrender of the whole spirit of the American people, who believed their destiny to be that of free arbitrators, and not partisans, in the future of civilisation; friends of liberty and democracy everywhere, and not allies on one side of a line. They had come into the war, they believed, as crusaders for that ideal, defenders of liberty wantonly attacked. They hated the thought that the ideal should be narrowed down to the future defence of one group of powers, who might in their turn attack or oppress the democratic liberties of their neighbours. For this reason, among others, they rejected the pact of security given by President Wilson to France in agreement with England. For these reasons, not ignoble or merely selfish—although, I think, unsound—they refused to enter the League of Nations.

This withdrawal of the United States took away the strongest pillar upon which the League had been founded. Its weakness was immediately apparent. It was incapable of world judgments backed by the greatest economic power in the world. The exclusion of Russia, Germany, Austria and Hungary from its deliberations and decisions made it seem—to hostile observers—an instrument designed merely as a partisan body, upholding the opinions of the victorious Allies and giving a sham morality to their policy.

That was unfair, because the Assembly, and its work behind the scenes at Geneva, in which forty-three nations were represented, did very quickly develop a spirit of international co-operation and law rising above the low moralities of national selfishness. The representatives of the League included large numbers of men who were passionately inspired with the purpose of restoring order into the chaotic conditions of Europe after war, healing its wounds, creating good will in causes of quarrel by methods of arbitration and persuasion, for the commonweal of peoples. The work and spirit of Geneva was one source of light in a world of darkness, in those dreadful years from which we have just emerged, and for that reason it raised a standard of idealism round which millions of men and women in many countries—even in the United States—rallied as the one hope of the future.

It may be said without exaggeration that for the six years following the war civilised humanity has been sharply divided into two camps of thought

—those who believe in the spirit of the League of Nations, with its message of international co-operation and its faith in peace by arbitration; and those who have no faith at all in this idealistic purpose, and who believe in Force as the only method of international relationship and the settlement of quarrels. Those two camps still exist. The argument between them still goes on, and will never cease until civilisation gives allegiance to a new code of law.

What frustrated the League in its work and decisions, after the withdrawal of the United States, was the interpretation of the Peace Treaties by the Great Powers, and the economic folly which took possession of European statesmen. The League as one half of the Peace Treaty found that its other half thwarted it in every possible way. The left hand worked against the right. It was useless for the League of Nations to press for the economic co-operation of Europe when the Supreme Council and the Allied statesmen enforced decisions which enlarged the area of ruin and thrust stricken people deeper into misery. It was futile for the League to discuss disarmament when France was building up a system of military alliances, creating a Black Army, and lending enormous sums of money to Poland and other States for maintaining their standing armies. It was almost hopeless for the League of Nations to offer its services for arbitration and to talk high moralities about international justice when, to avenge the murder of some officers by unknown assassins, Italy bombarded Corfu, killing innocent children; and when Italy and France were secretly conniving with the Nationalist Turks for a war against Greece, which was abandoned in its agony to the horror of Smyrna.

THE FRANCE OF POINCARÉ

France, under the leadership of Poincaré, scoffed from the beginning at the League of Nations, although supporting it over the Corfu incident, and although one representative, M. Léon Bourgeois, was a loyal friend of the League idea. After the refusal of the United States to ratify the pact of security for France against another war of German aggression, followed by the withdrawal of Great Britain, the France of Poincaré saw no safety except in the power of her Army in alliance with other forces which she could link in a military chain around her defeated enemies. No one ought to blame France for that philosophy, in view of her agony and her future peril. But it resulted inevitably in actions which checked the recovery of Europe, aroused all the old hatreds, filled the defeated peoples with a sense of profound injustice, and raised the old devils of national pride, vengeance, and belief in force which for a time had been banished to the houses of the German Junkers and had lain low in German hearts. It was the cause of increasing friction, spasms of passionate ill-will, between France and England, and a long campaign of scurrilous abuse in the French Press which poisoned the old Entente Cordiale, wiped out the memories of war comradeship, and was a tragic and painful chapter in recent history.

France under Poincaré demanded her pound of flesh from Germany, including the lifeblood of the German people in the arteries of its economic health. Germany could not recover nor, before recovering, pay. Afterwards, when the Ruhr was invaded, their chief source of wealth and of payment was strangled. The French objects of "security" and "reparations" were in hopeless an-

tagonism, and defeated each other. There could
be no reparations, on a large scale, if French security demanded the expulsion of those who directed and worked the Ruhr and its railways.
There could be no "security" for France in the
long run if, instead of German reparations, she
goaded the German people into nationalism and
a war of vengeance by every means, fair or foul.
While the policy of Poincaré was dominant,
Europe sank deep into despair, and the nations
most stricken by war saw no hope of revival.

The first three years after the World War provided terrible proofs of the disaster which had
happened to humanity in that deadly struggle.
Those who wish to convince the future generations
of the devastating effect of modern warfare upon
highly organised nations, as a frightful warning,
must summon up the picture of Europe in 1919,
1920 and 1921. I saw it from end to end, and it
haunted me.

THE RUSSIAN REVOLUTION

On the Eastern side of Europe Russia was cut
off from the family of nations and lay prostrate.

Civilisation itself had gone down there in anarchy
and misery, and its new government of Bol-
sheviks was ruling over a hundred million people:
hungry, diseased, stricken, crushed in spirit, weak
in body, overcome by melancholy and inertia. They
had broken first under the strain of war. Four
million of their men had died in the fields of
slaughter and their labour had been taken from
the fields. Corruption beyond words, treachery
in high places, inefficiency amounting to murder,
had aroused a spirit of revolt amongst soldiers
sent forward without arms to fight against men
with whom, individually, they had no lasting cause
of quarrel; peasants like themselves, gun-fodder
like themselves, for ambitions and hatreds which
they did not share. They turned to rend their
own leaders and made a pact at any price with
the enemy outside. All the explosive forces of
passion which had been stored up in centuries of
tyranny by a brutal Tsardom and its Governors
burst out against its present representatives,
although the last Tsar was a gentle man who
loved his people. Old dreams of liberty, new
philosophies of democracy, united for a time to
overthrow the Government and all its powers.

[109]

Revolution, bloody and cruel, raged in Russia, and the beast leapt up in peasant minds. Kerensky tried to control this anarchy but was swept on one side like a straw by stronger forces. Lenin and his crowd took command, and their new philosophy of Communism, fair-sounding, theoretically righteous, based upon the principles of equality and brotherhood and peace, put a spell upon the simple minds of the Russian folk. All opponents, critics, doubters, were destroyed relentlessly. Lenin and his friends, having taken command of the new machinery of Government by Soviet committees, were in supreme power over a people unarmed, half-starving, and submissive to those who had broken their old chains. It was some time before the Russian folk were aware of the fetters which enslaved them, and of a tyranny over their minds and bodies more ruthless than that of Tsardom. They were denied freedom of speech, freedom of knowledge, freedom of movement. The newspapers published the news of the world according to Lenin. The schools taught economic history according to Karl Marx and world history according to Soviet philosophy. Trotsky fashioned a Red Army in which discipline was more severe than

[110]

under the Grand Duke Nicholas. The prisons were filled with people of all classes who came under the notice of the secret police. Execution became a habit. There was a Reign of Terror undoubtedly as bad as that of the French Revolution of 1793.

For a time the people as a whole were keyed up to a new enthusiasm for what they believed to be a democratic system of Government by attacks from the "White Armies" of the old Royalists, financed, armed and organised by foreign powers, and especially by France and Great Britain. As Republican France had risen against the armies of the *emigrés,* so Soviet Russia rallied against the armies of Koltchak, Denikin, Wrangel and others, and defeated them overwhelmingly. After that the Reign of Terror abated somewhat, internal revolt died down, and the gospel of Communism was seen at work in conditions of peace.

It failed to work. It was all very well for the Communists to hand out tickets for bread, clothes, boots, education and operas to all those who were registered for service to the State, but those who presented the tickets found that there was not enough bread to go round, that no clothes or boots were forthcoming, that education is a poor thing on

[111]

empty stomachs in schools where the teachers died of starvation, and that the opera, beautiful as it continued to be, was not nourishing after a day of hunger. The workers fled from the factories because they could get no food. In the fields the peasants resisted the soldiers who tried to requisition their grain for the cities. Transport broke down. Grass grew on the railways. Horses and cattle died for lack of fodder. Typhus was rampant for lack of soap, medicines, decent conditions of life. Then famine struck the Volga region after two summers of drought. Twenty-five million people were threatened with death by actual starvation, and all over Russia there were hunger, fear, and despair.

From the famine districts the roads were black with fugitives moving to districts where they hoped to find food, while, from those very districts, people were trekking away from barren fields. Parents abandoned their children. When I went down the Volga the people were eating dried leaves, chopped straw and clay. The children were dying. The old people awaited death. And far away in Petrograd and in Moscow the factories were deserted, the hospitals were stone cold for lack of fuel, and there was not a single man or woman who had any comfort of body or soul.

Communism had failed. Its failure was proclaimed by Lenin himself. Russia was *in extremis* after a war which had broken the machinery of its life and a revolution which had failed to fulfil any of its promises, except equality—in misery.

That downfall of Russia was the worst thing in Europe, and was the cause of some of its general poverty. Trade was cut off from a hundred million people. Their purchasing power had been extinguished, so that neighbouring countries could not sell to them. Their own sources of wealth had perished, so that neither wheat nor oil nor flax could be exchanged for manufactured goods. The wealth of the world was so much less.

At that time the new Baltic States were unable to support themselves on any decent standard of life. Their children also were underfed. No trade came into the port of Riga, which once had been busy with the world's merchandise.

In Poland there was the spiritual warmth of national independence, but not much else. Misery was widespread. Food for the army was taken from the people. Commerce was stagnant, industry at a standstill. Germany was not buying from Poland. Poland could not buy from Germany or Russia. Underneath its new military ardour there was desperate need in the homes of the workers.

THE AGONY OF AUSTRIA

In Austria there was utter hopelessness, and the health of the people was breaking down. The Reparations Commission, under Sir William Goode, established to exact indemnities, saw the folly of such action and became a Relief Mission to save the lives of those people, the most charming and brilliant and civilised in Central Europe, before they sank under the doom pronounced upon them by a Treaty of Peace which had left them with the capital city of a great Empire from which the Empire had been lopped. I went into the Austrian hospitals, homes, babies' crèches, and children's clinics, and saw little Austrian children so weak from under-nourishment that they could not sit up in bed and crippled with rickets. Children of three and four had no solid bone in their

[114]

bodies, but only gristle. Where their arms were crossed at night there were deep sunken hollows. Sixty-eight per cent. of the Austrian children were in a state of semi-starvation in the year that followed war.

THE GERMAN PEOPLE

In Germany it was not so bad—but bad. For the last year of the war the people had been reduced to the bare limits of food supply. After the war, when the blockade was maintained until the signature of peace, the children went without milk and fats and there was general shortness of provisions, not amounting to actual starvation, but weakening the working men and women. Factory workmen told me that they never ate meat, and existed on bread and potatoes. It was enough for life, they said, but not enough for physical strength. They felt tired. Women fainted in the tramcars. There was stinting and scraping in every home, except those of the "profiteers," who by some genius of finance were making a good thing out of the fall of the mark.

[115]

Coming across Europe like that, and seeing the spreading track of financial and commercial ruin, the lowering of the standard of life in many countries where it had been high and splendid, the loss of purchasing power for anything but the barest necessities, and all the new frontiers and customs lines between new States and old States, checking the free interchange of goods, slowing down world trade, an observer like myself was staggered by the gravity of this state of things. It seemed to me that we were all heading for disaster. I was convinced that all those fair promises of quick prosperity, German reparations, revival of British trade, stabilising of international exchanges, would be utterly falsified unless there was a new co-operation among the countries of Europe on lines of economic common sense, and a truce to the policy of demanding from the defeated countries immense sums of money beyond their ability to pay. It seemed to me very clear that if Germany went down into real economic disaster the whole of Europe would go down too, and that what was wanted most was not payment of fantastic reparations but a return to the normal exchange of goods and energy. I was afraid for England.

[116]

THE UNCERTAIN PEACE

The British Government, after the armistice and the uncertain Peace, had behaved for a while as though victory had re-established her old strength. Superficially, indeed, and in moral prestige, among the nations of the world, the British Empire had emerged stronger than before the war. The menace of the German fleet was at the bottom of the sea. New territories in Africa had come under British dominion. British spheres of influence had been extended through Palestine, Mesopotamia and Persia. But those new "mandates" were a source of weakness and not of power. They were very costly at a time when there was no money to spend on new adventures in Imperialism. At least the vast sums of money poured into Mesopotamia and other Eastern territories on extravagant administration and development could not be justified to British tax-payers confronted by a staggering bill of costs for war purposes which drained the old reserves of wealth. British statesmen, not yet taught the elementary lessons of economic law, behaved with a kind of splendid madness, as though a new Golden Age had arrived in which their peo-

[117]

ple would possess an Oriental Empire such as Alexander had carved out of the old world. They forgot, or did not know, that poverty and something like industrial ruin was creeping over English life. They did not realise that after a devastating war they could not call upon the last reserves of manhood to support military adventures in far lands. They did not understand that the effects of war in Europe from the Rhine to the Volga, and beyond, had so lowered the purchasing power of the defeated peoples, the neutral countries and the new States, that Great Britain, for a long time to come, would lose many of her old markets for the export trade upon which her life depended, as well as the shipping of the world's merchandise from port to port which had been so great a source of her old wealth. Winston Churchill, with his restless imagination and wide-reaching Imperialism, dreamed dreams of British rule extending from the Cape to Cairo and from Tooting to Tibet. Even Lloyd George, for a little while, was intoxicated with the magnificence of the victory in which he claimed a chief share, not to be denied in history, in spite of some blunders and a feud with the Army Chiefs.

[118]

THE UNCERTAIN PEACE

THE LESSON OF REALITY

Then, quicker than in France, all this illusion was smashed in the face by reality. The British nation became aware of its dwindling trade, the stagnation of its industry. Unemployment began to creep up in a steady tide, until two million men were out of work and existing only on Government "doles." Factories were closing down or working half time. The Mersey, the Clyde and the Thames were crowded with ships without cargoes, and all the ports were filled with seamen without berths. After demobilisation ex-officers as well as men could not find jobs to do. They tramped the streets in search of work, wearing out their boots and their hearts. They played piano-organs, moved in dismal processions with banners flying the words "We want work," shook street collecting boxes in the faces of the passers-by. The Trade Unions were hard and selfish. They refused to admit untrained labour to their ranks. Without Trade Union tickets men who had saved the country were turned away at the factory gates. Labour put up a fierce fight to maintain the standard of wages and of life which had been established in

[119]

time of war—no longer possible in time of peace with failing markets and a world in ruin. One cannot blame them. None of us likes to reduce his standard of life and go back to miserable conditions of stint and scrape. Strikes and lockouts beat them down, but did not relieve the strain or increase the nation's wealth. Things looked very serious below the surface of English life. There was a bitterness in the minds of men who had been promised great rewards for heroic service, and now found themselves destitute, in overcrowded slums —where were the "homes for heroes"?—maintained on a miserable "dole" that just saved them from starvation but was not enough for decent life. There was for a year or so a danger of revolt, a spreading of revolutionary ideas, among men like that. Russian Communism put a spell upon many minds who knew nothing of the agony in Russia but were stirred by the Bolshevik doctrine of equality and the "dictatorship of the proletariat."

When Germany failed to pay the immense reparations which had been demanded from her the British Government was faced with the necessity of balancing its yearly Budget without those payments, and, unlike France, which still banked upon them, or like Germany, which created false money by inflation, determined to sustain the national credit by taxation and sound finance. It put the most tremendous burden upon the nation that has ever been sustained by any people in modern history. It was accepted with a resignation and courage which will stand for ever to the credit of the British folk, and especially to the credit of those who paid at the cost of all that was dearest to them in life apart from national honour and family blood. Income Tax, Super Tax, and Death Duties fell upon the people who lived on inherited wealth with a terrifying ferocity. There are only two and a half million people in Great Britain who pay any Income Tax at all, and only eighty-five thousand who are subject to Super Tax, but it was from that small minority that the Government demanded the revenue necessary for the upkeep of its services. It caused, and is causing, a social revolution which is changing the whole aspect of English life. The old aristocracy are abandoning their houses, selling their estates, becoming shabby genteel, losing their old splendour, prerogatives and power. To pay their Income

Tax and Death Duties they are eating into their old capital, selling the old pictures on their walls, abandoning old mansions haunted by the ghosts of history in which their pride and spirit dwelt. They have done this not without anguish, not without a sense of tragedy, not without bitterness, but with an acknowledgment of inevitable necessity. Bloodlessly the revolution in England is being accomplished, though the hard road has not yet been travelled to the end.

THE PRICE OF WAR

More crippling in its effects upon the nation as a whole was the taxation of capital in trade and industry. At a time when it was most necessary to limit the costs of production and to stimulate the adventure of trade, the business world was crushed under a burden of taxation which limited its reserves, put heavy charges upon the cost of manufacture, and reduced the capital available for new enterprise. The price of war, and of victory, lay with an almost intolerable weight upon the spirit of the British people, even before they had to shoulder the burden—rejected by every other nation—the payment of War Debt to the United States of America, amounting to £35,000,000 sterling every year. With an export trade less than 75 per cent. of what it reached before the War, with a population which had increased by nearly two millions in spite of all the slaughter, with new and ruinous expenses, and with a higher standard of life demanded by the labouring class, the people of Great Britain breathed hard, became very anxious, faced up to realities, and saw, with almost blinding clarity of vision, that their own national life depended upon the peace and recovery of Europe, including that of Germany and the defeated peoples. This realisation changed their whole attitude of mind towards the problem of peace. It made them draw farther and farther away from the French policy of Poincaré, which was based upon the prevention of German recovery and "security" by military force. But above all these financial considerations England believed in fair play even to a defeated foe, in generosity rather than vengeance, and in future peace by conciliation rather than by a military combination which one day would be challenged in another "inevitable" war, more ghastly than the last. All that sounded

[123]

like weakness and treachery to the mind of
France. The Entente Cordiale was strained and
broken . . .

PHYSICAL RECOVERY IN EUROPE

In many ways the recovery of Europe was more
rapid in its fundamental needs of life than seemed
possible after the devastation of war. Human energy, faith and hope repaired the material damage
of war in an almost miraculous degree. Walking
day by day across the battlefields of France and
Flanders it seemed impossible to me and to all
others that the ground upheaved by high explosives, criss-crossed with deep trenches, and sown
with unexploded shells would return within the
lifetime of the present generation to harvest fields
and pleasant pasture. It was incredible that all
those villages blown off the map, so that there were
only rubbish heaps to mark their site, should be
rebuilt within half a century with new walls and
sheltering roofs for the people who had fled from
them.

I never expected to see a new city of Ypres,
or to walk past shop windows in Arras, or to see a

[124]

harvest gathered on the outskirts of a new Peronne. The infernal track of war from Belgium to Switzerland, littered with dead bodies and the wreckage of battle, could not be wiped out, I thought, from the eyes of living men. But that has happened at least along some parts of the line ten years after. There are red roofs and busy streets in Ypres and Arras. The fields are smooth and green around Peronne. There are houses at Passchendaele. It is difficult to see the scars of war in Amiens. It is hard to find trenches and dug-outs or places where monstrous battles happened beyond the Menin Gate of Ypres or down by Lens, beyond the Vimy Ridge. Peasants dug out the unexploded shells. The trenches silted in or were ploughed in. The Belgians were as busy as bees when they returned to the hive. French contractors hired Poles and Czechs to supplement their French labour and made enormous fortunes in the reconstruction of destroyed towns at the cost of the French Government, which accepted all their claims until an orgy of corruption broke all bounds. In East Prussia, destroyed by Russian cavalry, little red houses were put up even more quickly because of German industry. In Italy many

[125]

wounds were hidden and healed. There is still much work to be done, especially in France, most terribly mutilated; but, ten years after, the work of reconstruction by the energy of men and women, desperate in their desire to blot out the years of agony and get back to peaceful labours and their old home life, is a splendid victory over the forces of destruction. Life triumphs over death, as always in history.

So also the stricken peoples staggered up from the bog of misery into which they were deep sunk after war. The land saved the cities, and the peasants found the source of life in the kind earth again. One nation above all helped them to tide over the lean years and live until they could reap new harvests. Without that rescue, millions more would have died and Europe would have been swept by pestilence and famine. The people of the United States did a work of charity on behalf of the starving folk of Europe, more especially in the rescue of the starving children, which absolves them, if they need absolution, from the charge of utter selfishness and indifference to the sufferings of that Europe from which they drew back in a policy of isolation.

THE UNCERTAIN PEACE

It is one of the paradoxes of recent history that while the American people, hardened against the Wilson ideal of co-operation with Europe, drew away from the League of Nations as an accursed thing with which they would have no part or lot, and reasserted the Monroe Doctrine with a new interpretation of narrow exclusiveness, they gave with their left hand, nearest to the heart, what their right hand refused. Publicly they said, "Let Europe stew in its own broth." Privately they poured out their dollars in charity for European relief.

THE "A.R.A."

Early in the War the American Relief Administration, organised by Herbert Hoover, fed day by day many millions of people in the areas of enemy occupation. A great deal of these food supplies was contributed by Great Britain, Canada, Australia, and other countries, as it is only fair to say, but the American contributions were enormous, and the organisation by American officials was a model of efficiency and zeal. As soon as the War ended, the A.R.A., as Hoover's administration was universally known, extended its operations and intensified its appeals to the charity of the American people on behalf of the stricken populations on both sides of the war zone. The American Government supported this work by immense subsidies of surplus stocks, which perhaps was good business as well as good will. But the good will was there, and it was reinforced by a volume of generosity which welled up from an almost inexhaustible source of private charity. The A.R.A. sent its officers and its food trains into Austria, Germany, Poland, Czecho-Slovakia, Serbia, Hungary, Armenia, Esthonia, Latvia, Lithuania, and many other countries. It established feeding centres and kitchens in the most necessitous cities and areas. It measured millions of children by a rough-and-ready system which showed the standard of under-nourishment and vital debility. It rushed food out to the innocent victims of war's cruelty, and helped, prodigiously, to save the world's childhood, without distinction of race, religion or politics. It was a divine work, inspired by God's love, after four years of hate and horror. In Europe other societies, like the Save the Children Fund, the Society of Friends, the Imperial Relief Committee, and the International Red Cross, did splen-

did work too, with less means and out of increasing
poverty, on behalf of all this mass of human suffering left as the heritage of war, but the A.R.A.
was the most powerful crusade of rescue, and by
its far-reaching aid did undoubtedly give the
stricken peoples time and chance to recover their
power of self-subsistence after a period when physical weakness, moral despair, and the ravages of
war had deprived them of the means of life above
the hunger line.

It was when famine took possession of the most
fertile territories of Russia that the A.R.A. did its
greatest work. In the United States of America,
as in England and France, the cry for help that
came out of Russia, so long cut off from human
intercourse, so long hidden by closed doors behind
which lay the tragedy of a great people, many men
and women, shocked to their inmost soul by stories
of Bolshevik atrocities, refused to listen to the voice
of charity. Many were certain that any food or
help sent to Russia would be used by the Communist leaders to save themselves from destruction or to support the Red Army and the Reign
of Terror. In any case, as some of them said,
why feed Russian peasants who have adopted the

[129]

pernicious philosophy of Bolshevism, or submitted
to it; and why feed Bolshevik babies who will grow
up to threaten the civilised code of decent peoples?
Let Russia pay the penalty of its atrocious crimes.

There was no country in the world where there
was a greater loathing of Bolshevism than in the
United States. It was to the majority of American citizens, as it is still, the Unspeakable Thing,
because it denied the rights of private property,
declared war upon Capital, and conspired for the
overthrow of all Governments based upon the Capitalist system. So much the more wonderful then
is the charity of those people who, with that enormous prejudice in their minds, heard the voice of
charity.

THE RUSSIAN FAMINE

I went into Russia with some of the first officials
of the A.R.A. and travelled with them to the Volga
region, where twenty-five million people were
threatened with starvation and starving. It was
Governor "Jim" of Indiana—Governor Goodrich
—whose wise, temperate and humane report was a
document which helped to save those millions. I

read it as he had written it in a slow-going train from Kazan to Moscow on the way back from dreadful scenes, and I gave the homage of my heart to that serene-eyed man who, with one lame leg, travelled through Russia on a diet of apples, went fearlessly into typhus-stricken places, and saw all things with a great pity, sound common sense, practical judgment, large humanity.

He was only an observer. Colonel Haskell and his little band of officers were the organisation and the administration in the field of action, of a great campaign of rescue which flowed out from America. They had to contend with the inertia of Russian character, with the suspicion of Soviet officials who feared a political purpose behind the work of charity, with a broken-down railway system, with no material for printing or packing, with immense distances and lack of transport, with the Russian language and bad interpreters, with Russian labour weakened by being under-nourished, and with millions of starving and disease-stricken people who had hardly the strength or will to help themselves or co-operate with others for their own rescue. It was a formidable adventure in which the young officers of the A.R.A.—like those of our

British relief societies—risked their lives by disease and were strained to the utmost of nervous energy. And they brought the food to Russia and distributed it to the starving folk. Millions died —Dr. Nansen reckons four millions—but eleven million people were fed every day by the A.R.A. for nearly a year. In addition to that mass relief, millions of food packages addressed to individuals in Russia by relations and friends in the United States reached the starving and distressed people outside the area of actual famine, and gave new hope of life to those who had been reduced to misery and despair in Petrograd, Moscow, and other cities. When we think of the organisation and labour required in time of war to feed our armies in the field, it is almost miraculous that eleven million Russian peasants could be supplied at a distance of 6,000 miles, after the breakdown of the very machinery of their life. History will record it as the greatest campaign of relief and international charity every attempted or achieved.

It is only right to say that, after the first suspicions had been overcome, the Soviet Government and its officials played fair and did all they could to facilitate this work. The food did reach the starving children and their parents. The railways and engines were repaired. Trucks were built. A new hope dawned in Russia, which learnt something from American methods of efficiency. The Reign of Terror had worn itself out, the actual practice of Communism was abandoned, the rights of private property and private trading were, to some extent, restored, a great shadow passed from the spirit of the people, and in many ways life became endurable after the years of agony. The utter failure of the Communist experiment was acknowledged by Lenin within Russia itself, though its propaganda and revolutionary doctrines were still used to stir up trouble in the outside world. Slowly the life of the Russian people staggered up from misery, and although there is still great distress in many districts and a new threat of famine, the ninety million peasants, controlled by a small body of Communists whose economic philosophy has no appeal for them, are getting a bare life out of the soil, with now and then a surplus of grain for export in return for manufactured goods. Even Russia is on the road to recovery.

Other countries revived, at least to the extent of providing their own means of subsistence, in peasant states like those of the new Baltic nations. Even international trade recovered some of its old activity in countries, like Czecho-Slovakia, newly carved out of the old Austrian Empire and successors to its sources of industrial energy. But it was impossible to hope for any general and complete recovery of trade conditions in Europe so long as there was no stability in the value of monetary exchange and no political peace. The printing presses in many countries were issuing paper money which had no reality behind it, and the time came when it proved worthless either for internal commerce or for foreign business. Russian roubles had long ceased to have any purchasing power. A million roubles brought from Moscow would not buy a glass of Schnapps in Riga.

THE RELIEF OF AUSTRIA

In Austria money went the same way. The Austrian kronen, unsupported by gold or goods, became a mockery in the markets of the world and in Vienna itself. The professional classes were dying of starvation, the middle classes were reduced to an extreme destitution; labour, paid false

[134]

wages, had no heart to work. Several loans granted by the British Government and others, after abandoning all immediate claims to "reparations," withered away in supporting crowds of needy officials and struggling with financial chaos. Austria declared itself a bankrupt State, appealing to the world for help; and at last her immense distress was recognised by all other States, and the League of Nations was entrusted with the task of administering a new loan of something like fifteen millions sterling, with a strict control of Austrian revenue, expenditure, taxation, and financial measures.

It was a lesson to the world of what may be done by good will and common sense rather than by political hatred and international hostility. As a foster child of the League of Nations, Austria recovered in a way which seemed beyond hope. As soon as her money was stabilised to a fixed value, because of its gold backing, trade began to flow back a little, capital came to the rescue, with a sense of security. The Austrian people were able to buy food in return for their merchandise at prices which no longer fluctuated wildly according to the downfall of paper money. They were able

[135]

to accept contracts for future work and to fulfil them with a certainty that the money they received would not melt in their hands like summer snow. They recovered hope, worth more than gold, and physical strength restored their mental and moral health. The nightmare lifted. The city of Vienna to-day, in spite of much poverty and a disappearance of its former luxury among the old classes who dwelt in the splendour of Imperial Courts, is as different from Vienna in 1920 as the day from the night. The Viennese, once the gayest people in Europe, have learnt to laugh again. There is music in the cafés once more. The streets are lighted again. The children are no longer weak with rickets. The bitter cup has passed from them, except for those who remember their former state, and the old world of the Austrian Empire that has gone down with all its pride.

THE PROBLEM OF GERMANY

Germany remained the great problem of Europe and the great peril.

After the war, when "something seemed to break in them," as a German wrote to me, they were for a time stunned and dazed by defeat. To German pride of race it seemed incredible, even in the face of dreadful facts, that they had lost everything for which they had fought and struggled with such desperate and stubborn will-power. After all their victories! After all that slaughter! *"Deutschland über Alles!"* Now they were in chains, hopeless and helpless, disarmed, under the heel of France, Britain, Belgium—done and down!

The military chiefs hid themselves in their castles—sullen, broken. They put all the blame on the German people. It was they who had blundered and had been defeated. The invincible German armies had never been defeated. Never! Only Ludendorff in an incautious book confessed the truth that he had not been able to hold the line against the overwhelming assault of the Allies. But his argument was the same. It was German will-power that had broken behind the lines. It was Bolshevism and Pacifism that had let down the fighting men. When the Peace Treaties were published the German people gasped and, for a time, despaired. They were confronted with conditions which would crush them for all time.

However hard they worked, all the profits of their labour would be seized by their enemies. However much they pinched, more would be demanded. There was no fixed sum which they could wipe out by stupendous effort, but only sums rising higher in fantastic figures for ever and ever. They were the bondslaves of the world.

That mood did not last, though it came back again. A new mood followed and buoyed them up for a year or two. They had lost the War, but they would show the world that they could win the peace. German genius, organisation, and industry would rise above even the monstrous penalties exacted by their enemies. They would capture the markets of the world, smash all competitors by an industrial war, regain their liberty and commercial power. The Krupp works which had made great guns and all the monstrous machinery of war converted their plant to the instruments of peace, produced ploughs, steam-engines, safety razors, cash registers, everything that is made of metal for the use of life. Every factory in Germany got to work again. There were no unemployed as in England, because the workers accepted low wages, and desired work almost as

much as bread in a fever of industrial energy, to
wipe out the War and build up the prosperity of
a peace. Defeat was better than victory in its
moral effect upon the German people. At least
they did not fall into that idleness, that craving
for gaiety, that moral lassitude and indiscipline
of spirit which overcame the victorious peoples.
When I went to Germany, several times after the
War, I was amazed at its energy and industry.
There were no scenes in Berlin like those in London, with processions of unemployed and innumer-
able beggars and crowds of loungers round the
Labour Exchanges. There was an air of activity
in Germany, startling and rather splendid. The
whole nation was working full steam ahead, and
the products of its industry were being offered in
the markets of the world at less than the cost price
of similar goods in England. It steadied them and
gave them a purpose in life.

And yet beneath this superficial appearance of
renewed prosperity and industrial power there was,
as I could see, something rotten. Misery was not
to be seen in the open, as in London, but it was
there, in middle-class homes and mean streets.
The whole of this new industrial adventure in Ger-

many was based upon underpaid and undernourished labour, upon cut-throat prices, and upon the temporary advantage of a falling exchange.

The German Government was tinkering with its money, speeding up the printing presses, issuing notes beyond the backing of real securities. The illusion of a Germany capturing the world's markets had no great basis of truth. The world markets had lost their purchasing power, however cheap were German goods. Russia was not buying much from Germany, nor Austria, nor Poland, nor Hungary, nor Turkey. Looking into the figures given me by experts—English as well as German —it seemed certain that there was an adverse trade balance against Germany when her national expenditure was reckoned with her revenue. The reparations she was beginning to pay, the deliveries in kind she was making to France, Belgium, and Italy, the costs of the Armies of Occupation on the Rhine, were eating into her capital wealth and swallowing up her last gold reserves. She had to pay her indemnities by buying foreign money— dollars, sterling, francs—and after each payment her own money depreciated by irresistible economic laws.

[140]

THE UNCERTAIN PEACE

THE ADVENTURE OF INFLATION

The financial advisers of the German Government used the method of inflation to keep the German people working on cheap money to avoid a revolution which they feared would happen if unemployment prevailed, to wipe out their internal debt, and to dupe the world. At first, no doubt, they believed that they could control this system of postponing the evil day of reckoning, but, once having started the ball rolling, it increased with frightful velocity down hill. Every time the mark fell in value more marks had to be printed. When its purchasing power fell so far below the real value of wages that the workers clamoured for increased pay, the printing presses had to be turned again to provide the additional money which again fell in the foreign exchange while more slowly prices rose in Germany. The German financiers never checked this wheel in its mad revolutions. They protested that they were unable to check it. To some extent it was a gamble with loaded dice. They were bound to win—up to a point. As long as foreign money was paid for worthless paper— whatever the figure of exchange—they would be

[141]

taking good money for bad, which is excellent business. As long as by increasing the quantities of paper they could enable their industrialists to employ cheap labour, it was good business. As long as the paper itself and the labour of printing were not more costly than the purchase value represented by fantastic numbers on the note, they could carry on the economic life of the country and at the same time abolish all their internal debts. People who had invested all their savings in war loans found that their income had withered away. Industrial companies who had borrowed real capital could pay it back in false notes. And private individuals who were ruined by this means could at least recoup themselves a little at the expense of the foreigner by selling German paper for pounds, dollars or francs, and gambling on the exchange. It was a great game, which absorbed the interest of large numbers of the German people. Waiters in hotels, clerks in offices, vendors of newspapers, middle-class housewives, did their little bit of daily speculation, and secreted foreign money for rainy days. The great industrialists and professional financiers speculated on a large scale and made enormous profits, while the game lasted. But it was a game bound to fail in the long run. It was bound to fail when no other country would buy German marks at any rate of exchange, and when those who possessed real things, such as potatoes, meat, milk, or manufactured articles, refused to part with them for any number of German notes. That time came during the occupation of the Ruhr, when, to subsidise the passive resistance of the workers, the German Government poured out a vast tide of paper money, and when the German nation was cut off from its chief source of real wealth in that great industrial region.

I saw from time to time the progress along the road to ruin. Although it enabled a minority to get rich quick, it caused intense suffering among the mass of the German people. The wages of the workers never kept pace with the fall in the purchasing power of their wages, although they were raised week by week on an ascending scale. What five marks would buy in 1913 a million marks would not buy in 1923. It made trade impossible, because no sooner were prices adjusted to the new note issues than a fresh burst of inflation made them less than the cost price of the goods a week before. It was futile to save when thrift

[143]

was mocked by this depreciation and disappearance of money values. German people had to spend quickly in food or drink or foolish things, because what they had to-day would be worthless to-morrow. The German housewife despaired. She could not keep pace with these rising prices. Some of them went crazy over millions of marks that had no meaning. Germany, apart from its profiteers, stinted, scraped, and toiled, without decent reward for its labour, and with certain ruin ahead.

Looking back on that amazing adventure of inflation, one must ask oneself the question what would have happened in Germany if its Government had endeavoured to stabilise its finances by not issuing money beyond its real backing, and trying to balance its Budget according to sound methods? It is my opinion that the illusion of German prosperity would have been more rapidly dispelled and that their default in the payment of reparations would have happened earlier. Foreign speculators would not have been "bitten in the ear," German speculators would not have made profits over exchange gambles; but the Allies would not have received more payments, and there would have been widespread unemployment and revolt among the German people. They were between the devil and the deep sea, and though they chose the devil of inflation it postponed the plunge into the deep sea for a year or two more.

In fairness to Germany it must be remembered that she did make very heavy payments in money and kind, amounting all told to more than £400,-000,000 sterling—that is to say, nearly half the amount of the British debt to the United States of America, which the British people, richer than Germany at the present time, find an almost intolerable burden, although they are paying only £30,000,000 a year to reduce it. In Germany's post-War state it was a drain upon her dwindling capital which she could not sustain at anything like that rate, and with or without inflation it crippled her. The Dawes Report was an acknowledgment of that fact, although it took into account the immense sums of money secreted abroad. Previous default had caused the French occupation of Dusseldorf, Duisburg, and Frankfurt, arousing a flame of hostility in German minds. But when France marched into the Ruhr against the will of the British and without their co-operation, the

[145]

whole of the German people, without difference of class or political opinion, denounced it as a violation of the Peace Treaty, and as a sentence of ruin, not only to Germany herself, but to the whole of Europe.

THE OCCUPATION OF THE RUHR

It was this occupation of the Ruhr—the threat of its happening, the entry of the French troops, and the results of it—which poisoned the relations between England and France, flung Germany back into the arms of her Nationalists, and thwarted all efforts of international good will in the spirit of the League of Nations. It kept the wounds of war open and salted in Central Europe. It checked the economic recovery of all nations dependent upon Germany as buyers and sellers. France failed to get her reparations, and instead of building up security the policy of Poincaré made a future war between the two nations almost inevitable by stirring a cauldron of boiling pitch. It turned the justice of the War into an injustice of peace, with the Germans as the victims of injustice. For how could they pay reparations if their industrial heart was strangled? And how could

[146]

they submit to a military tyranny over their great working population from an enemy which had professed to fight the war for liberty and democracy? How could any peace be justified which enabled a foreign army, after war, to hold up the chief industries of a great country, to destroy the machinery of its life, to coerce its workers at the point of the bayonet, to expel them when they refused to work under their military command, to take their money, to fling out their furniture, to imprison their working chiefs, to cut off their food supplies, to prevent their intercourse with their own folk, to deal with the passive resistance of proud and hungry men as though it were a crime against France, to use their whips in German theatres, to terrorise the inhabitants of a great district, to break their spirit by a thousand tyrannies, insults, humiliations and brutalities? That was how the Germans argued, and the argument stands in the soul of Germany as a memory that must one day be wiped out in blood. I think France under Poincaré was unwise in giving to Germany that sense of injustice and that cause of vengeance. I think France under Herriot thinks so too, although it cannot forget, as none of us can forget, the abom-

inable acts of German officers and men during time
of war in France and Belgium.

The argument on the French side was logical
enough, to a certain point, where its logic broke
abruptly. France, as its mind was expressed by
Poincaré, said: "These people have not paid us.
They are not trying to pay us. They are in wilful
and flagrant default."

They paid no attention to the German reply
that they had paid all they could—enormous sums
—and could pay no more without utter ruin. In
any case, they did not yet know the fixed sum of
their debt, and the figures France demanded were
beyond the capacity of any nation on earth.

"Very well," said the French, "we will take
pledges for future payment. We will send the
bailiff into the house; we will hold the Ruhr until
Germany realises the inevitable and makes better
arrangements to pay. Meanwhile, whether she
pays or not, we shall weaken her power of recovery, postpone the time when she is able to challenge
us again, and hold her by the throat for the security
of France. Excellent plan, both ways! Perfectly
justified in law and equity."

Where France failed in logic was in the combination of two ideas which were mutually destructive. She might gain military security (for a time) by weakening Germany and keeping a grip on her jugular vein, but she could not gain reparations at the same time and by the same method. Above all, her logic on the point of security would fail at some future date—twenty years, forty years, sixty years, when the German people would be strong enough to fight for the liberty of their life, by the mere weight of increasing population inspired by passion and armed with new weapons. France would have done better to seek the security of world opinion in support of her just claims instead of risking this lonely adventure against the judgment of her friends. That, I think, was the verdict of the Dawes Report. It was certainly the verdict of British opinion among moderate-minded folk, long before the Ruhr episode had ended in the financial downfall of Germany and explosive passion.

THE GERMAN SEPARATISTS

What further excited the bitter hatred of the Germans was the effort of French generals and

[149]

political agents to detach the loyalty of the Rhineland from the German Empire by encouraging bodies of "Separatists," who proclaimed a Rhineland Republic. Led by a very doubtful but plausible gentleman named Dr. Dorten, whom I met in the early days of the British occupation, these "Separatists" were mostly youths of the disorderly class and men of criminal type supported by a few sincere fanatics. Many of them were in the pay of the French. Their movement was regarded as black treachery by patriotic Germans, and when the French troops stood by the Separatists while they seized public buildings and murdered German police, previously disarmed by French orders, fury was unrestrained among the German people. French policy, in this matter at least, was a blunder, because from the first the Separatist movement had no basis of reality nor any chance of success. It was an illusion of French politicians who let their wish be father to their thoughts.

"THE BLACK HORROR"

Another cause of hatred in Germany, amounting to a mad rage which made them see red, was the

[150]

use of coloured troops in the French zone of occupation. Under the name of "The Black Horror," German propaganda exaggerated and falsified the hideous aspects of this last humiliation to their pride. It was asserted that masses of African negroes had been let loose in the Rhineland to assault white women and brutalise white men. The French denied that they were using any black troops, and this was perhaps technically true, although I saw with my own eyes Seneghalese negroes on the banks of the Rhine. But they were not fighting troops. They were transport men, lorry drivers, and ambulance drivers, in the blue uniform and steel hat of the French *poilu*. I saw the inhabitants of Bonn shudder and sicken at the sight of them. But it was true that the French did employ large numbers of Moroccan soldiers in German towns. They were not black, they were not even "nearly black," and in race they belonged to the same Mediterranean peoples from which the French themselves have sprung. But that made no difference in German psychology, and I sympathise with their detestation of being controlled and put under the menace of Moroccan troops who, whatever shade their colour and historical

[151]

ancestry, do not belong to our European type of
civilisation, such as it is, and should not be put in
military power over European populations. The
British use of Indian troops in the white man's
war, and the American use of black battalions,
were, in my judgment, similar errors which may
cost us dear. But it was more than an error to
use Moroccans in time of peace among German citizens who resented their presence as a shameful insult. These things are beyond argument. They
belong to the realm of instinct. It was handing
the Germans another cause of hatred.

BRITISH POLICY AND FRENCH SUSPICION

Most people in England watched all these things
with disapproval and dismay. Gradually, as time
went on, they drew further away from the French
policy in Europe. It seemed to them bad business
and bad morality. From a business point of view
a great number of hard-headed people in Great
Britain could see no sense in demanding payments
from Germany beyond her power to pay, and in
holding her by the throat so tightly that in any case
she could not pay. Unemployment and bad trade

in Great Britain were seen to be directly caused by this situation in Germany, which at one time had been England's second best customer. It was not only the direct trade between Germany and England that had declined, but it was the indirect effect of Germany's economic downfall all round the world. If Germany bought less wool from Australia and less grain from Canada, then Australia and Canada bought less manufactured goods from Great Britain. If Germany were not trading profitably with Holland, Denmark, and Sweden, then those countries could not buy the same quantity of British goods. Germany was the axle-tree of the great wheel of European trade which had broken its spokes and lay in the ditch. Until the old waggon was on the road again England would not recover her commerce. The French cried: "What about our devastated regions? Who will pay for reconstruction if the Germans are not forced to do so?" The English shrugged their shoulders and said: "What about our devastated trade in Liverpool, Manchester, Glasgow, London, and a hundred other cities where men are out of work?"

Less than ten years after the beginning of that

struggle in which the youth of these two countries had fought side by side for the same purpose, and with the same ideals, there was a friction between England and France which obliterated the memory of that common sacrifice in many minds and created suspicion, dislike and political hostility.

The French Press and people abused the British for their materialism. "That nation of shopkeepers!" they cried. "They can think of nothing but their trade interests. They would sell their soul or their best comrade for a mess of pottage!" They forgot that they also were out for financial interests, that their policy was dictated by the desire to get reparations out of Germany. And although England advanced commercial reasons for relieving the pressure on Germany, she had other reasons which to the French seemed sheer hypocrisy, the most sickening cant. The English people and their sister nations do not like kicking an enemy when he is down, nor treading on his face when he lies prostrate. The old traditions of sport, strong even in the Cockney mind, bid them shake hands with the other fellow when he has been counted out after a knock-out blow. They do not believe in "hugging hate." They have an instinc-

[154]

tive sense of fair play. It is not too much to say that these were the overwhelming reasons in the minds of the average Englishman which made him dislike the entry into the Ruhr and the Poincaré policy of "keeping the Germans down."

LLOYD GEORGE AND POINCARÉ

There was another reason, deep in many minds of humble folk and great statesmen. They looked back to the War with loathing and horror. They desired to support some better way of argument in international disputes, so that there need be no "next war," worse than the last, between the same combination of Powers. They believed in the spirit of the League of Nations as the only way by which that next war might be avoided. They were hostile to any Power which seemed to thwart the progress of that spirit. They believed that the policy of Poincaré was contrary to the establishment of good will among nations. They believed that it was hurtful to future peace and leading inevitably to a war of revenge. For that reason millions of people in Great Britain looked upon Poincaré and all he stood for as the greatest menace in the world.

[155]

Lloyd George was one of them. After the signing of the Peace Treaty and a jingo election in which his followers appealed to the lowest passions of the people, that extraordinary man with his nimble mind, his rapid vision, his instinctive Liberalism, his sincere belief in righteousness (overlaid by the cunning and craft of political necessities), led him into a crusade on behalf of a world settlement by conciliation and compromise.

In conference after conference, with splendid courage, with untiring zeal, with broad and liberal views, with an honest desire to bring Europe back to health by fair play all round and business methods, he endeavoured to settle the differences between France and England over this question of Germany, to scale down the German payments so that they were possible and not impossible, to give France security, to bring Russia back into the family of nations, to make some reasonable arrangement for inter-allied debts, and to adopt a scheme of general demobilisation in Europe which would relieve its peoples from crushing burdens and prepare the way of peace. However one may criticise the character and quality of Lloyd George, history will, I think, give him enormous credit for that

[156]

great endeavour to secure the peace of the world. At every conference he was thwarted by France, whose difficulties and dangers could not be reconciled by any of these plans, who regarded them all as treachery to her people.

Briand concluded an agreement by which he released Germany of certain obligations in return for a limited guarantee of French security by British alliance in the case of a new aggressive war from Germany. And with that document in his pocket Briand lost his job in France. Poincaré succeeded him as the representative of French nationalism, the military point of view, the unrelenting will of the majority of French people to exact their full pound of flesh from Germany at all costs. From that time onwards until the downfall of Lloyd George himself the situation between France and England was controlled by the diplomatic intercourse between Lloyd George and Poincaré which developed into a personal duel of hostile views. In every case Poincaré had the best of the argument on lines of pure logic and abstract justice. It was right that Germany should pay for all the damage she had done. Was France to pay? . . . In every conference Poincaré stone-

[157]

walled Lloyd George's attempt at compromise, by
which logic should give way a little to general interest and the military safety of France to a world
pact of peace.

Then Lloyd George fell. By a frightful para-
dox his fall was partly due to a call for war. The
man who was passionate for the peace of the world,
who had given his health and risked his political
career in the cause of the pacification of Europe,
raised a fiery torch to the people—which fell like
a damp squib in a cold sea. It was after the tragedy of Greece.

For some reasons not yet fully known to history, Lloyd George had fallen under the spell of
Venizelos and his friends. Greece had been given
a new Empire in Asia Minor and Thrace at the
expense of the Turk, who had been utterly crushed
by British armies. He turned a deaf ear to all
critics who prophesied that the character of the
Greeks would not be equal to these new responsibilities.

THE DOWNFALL OF GREECE

Meanwhile in Constantinople, where I happened
to be, our Military Mission was getting anxious.

[158]

THE UNCERTAIN PEACE

A new leader had arisen among the Turks named Mustapha Kemal Pasha. Established at Angora, with a Committee of Turkish Nationalists, he defied the terms of peace imposed upon his people, refused to acknowledge the decree of a Sultan in the hands of the inter-allied force, rallied to his standard every Turkish patriot, raised a new army, filled Constantinople with his spies and agents, and proclaimed a "Holy War" of Islam. He vowed to recapture Smyrna, to liberate Constantinople, and to take possession of Thrace.

The Greek troops before Smyrna were confident, as I saw them, of holding their lines against the Turk. The Greek Commander-in-Chief, whom I interviewed, was ready to break the Turkish lines "as though on parade." Lloyd George gave them the moral support of emotional words, and they were very grateful to him, and believed that England was behind him. The world knows what happened. Its conscience must still burn at times as it hears the cries of terror and anguish on that quayside at Smyrna when the Turkish irregulars set fire to the Christian quarters and massacred men, women and children, while British and American warships stood by, with their officers and men staring through that pall of smoke and its rending fire, listening to the shrieks beyond.

The Turks advanced to the Ismid Peninsula overlooking the Dardanelles. They advanced to the very lines which the British troops—young boys mostly—held at Chanak. Beyond that they could not go without a war with Great Britain, which hung by a thread day after day and week after week. The French, whose politicians and public opinion were sympathetic to the Turks, and who were incredibly jealous of British influence in Egypt, Palestine and Mesopotamia—an old source of enmity stirred up again in military minds— withdrew their own troops from Chanak, and left the British troops isolated. They made it perfectly clear, very courteously, but very firmly, that they would not engage in war against Turkey. It is certain that the French people after all their loss of blood and years of strife would have refused to support such a war. In any case, they preferred the Turks to the Greeks, and were glad of the Greek defeat.

To Lloyd George, in England, these Turkish victories were heavy blows. His honour was engaged to Greece. He believed that British honour

was engaged, though certainly his pro-Greek policy had never gained the support and enthusiasm
of public opinion. He hated the thought of seeing
the Turk in power again at Constantinople. He
had incited the Greek Army to attack. The horror
at Smyrna made his blood run cold. It was Winston Churchill, without waiting for Parliamentary
sanction, who raised the fiery cross and sent an
emotional appeal for help to all the Dominions.
It was received at first in stony silence, and then
with deadly hostility. Neither Canada nor Australia would send a man to fight in a new war.
They had done enough, they were not interested.
At home in England and Scotland there was no
support for a new war. There was a fierce outcry
in the Press. The nation refused to envisage war,
for any reason. They were sick of war. They
could not afford it in men or money after years
of colossal sacrifice.

The war did not happen, thanks a good deal to
General Sir Charles Harington, commanding in
Constantinople. Cool as ice in the face of extreme
provocation, determined to keep the peace by every
method of statesmanship, unless his men were actually attacked, it was his fine chivalry, his diplomatic

[161]

wisdom with the Turkish Generals and statesmen, which resulted in an armistice hanging on a hair-trigger. Lord Curzon patched up a peace which gave to the Turks most of what they claimed and more than they ought to have had in humanity and justice. The expulsion of the Christian communities from Asia Minor was one of the most infernal tragedies of history, hushed up in the British and European Press because it hurt the conscience of too many of us. The flight of the Greek refugees still calls to God for pity. . . .

What a world—ten years after!

THE DENIAL OF DEMOCRACY

When I went about Europe I was dismayed by the denial of all mental progress towards a state of peace. Physically there was a slow recovery from war. Morally there was a reaction in many countries to black passion, militarism, and ideas of Force. Austria-Hungary and Germany were swinging right back to the old traditions of nationalism. They saw no way of freedom except by future war. They desired vengeance—against the French. They were talking of calling back their Emperors. In Germany the Crown Prince came home as a "private citizen" ready for a call to the throne at some not distant date. The war which was to make the world safe for democracy had been followed by a peace in which democracy was repudiated by many leaders and by public opinion in many countries. "I do not believe in democracy," Herr Streseman told me in Berlin. The Italian Fascists under Mussolini did not believe in democracy, nor in Parliamentary institutions, nor in free speech. They bludgeoned men who disagreed with their ideas and methods or poured castor oil down their throats. They saved Italy from anarchy, which was a good deed, but Mussolini, the autocrat, was quite willing to play the anarchist against international laws and did so when he flouted the League of Nations and bombarded Corfu. Students of world affairs, thoughtful observers like Sir Edward Grey and General Smuts, men not given to exaggerated speech and morbid fears, expressed their alarm at the state of Europe ten years after the outbreak of the World War, and confessed that it seemed to be slipping downhill towards general catastrophe.

[163]

TEN YEARS AFTER

THE REVIVAL OF HOPE

Since then something has happened to change the outlook of Europe and renew the hopes of peace. It is the London Agreement by which Germany, France, Great Britain, Belgium, and Italy agreed on Saturday, August 16—ten years and fourteen days after the beginning of the World War—to accept the chief provisions of the Dawes Report for the restoration of German credit by international loans and to establish a business settlement of the reparations problem with German consent. As Ramsay MacDonald, Labour Prime Minister, said at the conclusion of the London Conference, this agreement was "the first Peace Treaty" since the end of the world conflict, "because we sign it with a feeling that we have turned our backs on the terrible years of war and war mentality."

Three great events in the political world led up to this new hope of peace and progress. The first was the friendly co-operation of the United States in the endeavour to find a business solution on the subject of German reparations. The second was the advent of a Labour Government in England.

[164]

THE UNCERTAIN PEACE

The third was the downfall of Poincaré, owing to a change of view in France which put Herriot into power as an opponent of the Poincaré school of thought.

AMERICAN IDEALISM

In the United States of America there had been a great searching of soul, turmoil, and even anguish of thought since the downfall and death of President Wilson. Although mass opinion had hardened against any European "entanglement" and any place in the League of Nations by which they would have to assume definite responsibilities, there was always an intellectual and combatant minority which protested against extreme "isolation" and a complete denial of co-operation with European nations for the sake of World Peace. In three separate lecture-tours in America, the last one from coast to coast, I saw something of the tug-of-war in the mind of the American people between the desire to escape from Europe and the wish to take a full share, even the world's leadership, in the reconstruction of civilisation and its progress towards the brotherhood of nations. On my second visit I saw a rising tide of idealism in favour of international service. On my third visit it was beating up still higher against walls of national selfishness, indifference and hostility. A great deal of the idealism was vague, verbose, unpractical, and without any definite goal. It was spread by the women's clubs, increasing in political activity and importance. It was expressed by many writers and lecturers, including those who had seen most of the war. It was discussed, heatedly, at every dinner table and at every "party" where well-read men and women gathered for conversation. Many financiers and business men, looking at foreign affairs with cold science, backed up the arguments of the idealists by saying that the United States ought to help to "straighten out Europe" for the sake of world trade and world peace. Many Generals and United States officers denounced war as an accursed thing, and prophesied the destruction of civilisation if another world war happened. Kinship with England, sympathy with France, made some Americans of the old stock sick at the thought of their national "selfishness"; though still, I think, the mass of the people were indifferent and bored and tired with regard to

[166]

Europe and its troubles. But the idealists, the women, the pacifists, the internationalists, the financiers, prodded up the indifference and brought pressure to bear on their Government. No "entanglements" certainly, but some policy of association with efforts for world peace. The Harding Administration, elected to keep America out of Europe, was timid and hesitating, but had good-will, and heard these voices at the door.

NAVAL DISARMAMENT

It was President Harding, with Charles Hughes as his Foreign Secretary, who summoned the Conference on Naval Disarmament, and carried it through with triumphant success, due not a little to the hearty co-operation of the British Government through its representative, Lord Balfour. That limitation of naval armaments was really the first step towards world peace, though many steps must follow before peace is secure. It did at least one enormous thing in history. It stopped the possibility of a competition in naval strength between Great Britain and the United States which, if it had happened, would not only have been a crush-

[167]

ing burden to the taxpayers but would have led inevitably to suspicion and hostility between our two nations. The agreement of Japan was also a check to a rivalry in naval power which would have produced explosive forces and passions. The agreement did not stop the possibility of naval warfare, but it killed its inevitability.

The conclusion of that conference re-inspired the idealists. It encouraged them to further efforts to stimulate public opinion. Mr. Charles Hughes suggested an economic conference in Europe which resulted eighteen months later in the acceptance of the Dawes Report. The women's clubs, the peace association, many of the leaders of American thought, became more and more distressed at the state of things in Europe, more and more convinced that only by American participation, at least in moral and economic spheres, could Europe solve its problems on lines of reasonable compromise.

AMERICAN SYMPATHY WITH FRANCE

The majority of Americans undoubtedly were in favour of the occupation of the Ruhr. They regarded Germany as a fraudulent debtor. They believed in the "strong hand." They had no patience, or very little, with the British view, which seemed weak and sentimental. Only the German-Americans, the Pacifists and the Socialists, with here and there bankers and business men and "intellectuals," believed that France was not giving Germany a fair chance, was thrusting Europe back into the mud and was violating the spirit of the League of Nations. This view changed a little, though imperceptibly, when France had entered the Ruhr and had failed to extract anything solid from that nation. Even the warmest sympathisers with the French point of view became a little tired of Poincaré's "No, no," to all arguments on behalf of compromise, and of his nationalistic utterances. American opinion, still hostile to Germany in the mass—more intolerant of German character, and more convinced of her exclusive war guilt than the British people who had suffered so hideously—swung away from the Poincaré policy, at least to the point of belief that the occupation of the Ruhr was no solution of the problem but only a method of enforcing a solution that had still to be found; and time was short. Germany's policy of inflation, that colossal fraud, had collapsed. Her

[169]

money was waste paper, her credit gone, her capacity to pay indemnities extinguished—for a time. Some international scheme, divorced from politics, conducted on strict business lines, must get at the real facts and impose a settlement, or Europe as well as Germany would go down in chaos, not without repercussion in the United States.

THE DAWES REPORT

It was with the will of the people, and an earnest desire to co-operate in this enquiry and report, that the American Government appointed General Dawes to the international committee which investigated the state of German finance and recommended a plan of action. It was another step towards American co-operation in the arrangement of world peace, and the beginning at least of a settlement in Europe based on business methods and common sense.

The Dawes Report cut like a clean wind through all sophistries, fantasies, illusions, and passions. It stated the realities, to France as well as to Germany. . . . Germany was a bankrupt State with great assets and immense potential energy. France and other countries could get heavy payments in course of time—if Germany were given industrial liberty and a loan to stabilise her monetary system, in securities which were good. Otherwise, they would get nothing. Take it or leave it. There were the facts.

The acceptance and working of the Report which disillusioned both France and Germany, and excited bitter opposition in both countries, was dependent on one incalculable element—goodwill on all sides. The German nationalists denounced it as an outrage, French nationalists as a surrender; Poincaré was prepared to discuss it subject to many reservations, including the occupation of the Ruhr and the military control of the Rhineland Railways. Not in that political atmosphere between the two nations was there a ghost of a chance for the Dawes Report.

But then two other events happened in the political world which by a kind of miracle changed the mental atmosphere of Europe, at least sufficiently to secure the adoption of the new scheme. They were the advent of the Labour Government in Great Britain and the downfall of Poincaré.

[171]

TEN YEARS AFTER

The Conservative Government under Baldwin, which succeeded the breaking-up of the Coalition under Lloyd George, deliberately committed suicide by appealing to the country for a mandate on Protection. Great Britain would have nothing of it at a time of unemployment, heavy costs of living, and diminishing trade. But the results of the election were unforeseen. The Conservatives lost their great majority, the Liberals were reduced to a minority, and Labour became the strongest single party in the new Parliament and received its call to office.

It was the greatest social revolution that has happened in England in modern history. The highest offices of state and of the very Court itself were occupied by men who had begun life in factories, mines and workships, or who had gained political notoriety by attack upon the privileges, traditions, social castes, and property rights of the most conservative country in Europe outside Spain. They were the leaders of that spirit of revolt which had surged below the surface of English life among ex-soldiers who had not received reward for serv-

[172]

ice, unemployed men who were living on poor doles, and of all those inarticulate millions who rallied to the Labour cause because it stood solidly and squarely for anti-militarism and world peace, for democratic liberties, and for ideals of a world state in which the common folk should have security, more pay for less work, more joy in life, and social equality levelled up to high standards of education and home comfort. Those I am sure were the instincts and hopes—not yet to be fulfilled!—which brought Labour into office.

They were there only on suffrance, and with guarantees of good behaviour. A combined vote of the Liberals and Conservatives could turn them out at any moment. But they played their cards cleverly, for a time, not adventuring on any revolutionary policy, not trampling on any old traditions, wearing Court uniform as though to the manner born, pleased with their prestige and power, being very polite to everybody, and keeping their hotheads quiet by promises of future reward when their majority would be substantial.

They were certainly lucky in having Ramsay MacDonald as their leader and Prime Minister. A man of high education, though humble birth,

[173]

with a fine dignity and grace of manner, sincere
in his ideals, believing in evolution and not revolution, and with an intimate knowledge of both foreign affairs and Parliamentary rules, he came as
no shock to the House of Commons, and inspired
admiration even among his political opponents.
Unable to do much to remedy the state of economic
life in Great Britain—even to fulfil his promises
regarding a remedy for unemployment—he concentrated all his efforts, wisely as well as tactfully,
on the endeavour to solve the European problem
between France and Germany. He saw at once
that it would never be solved as long as hostility
and suspicion embittered the relations of France
and England. The man whom all England had
accused as Pro-German wrote the most charming
and conciliatory letters to Poincaré, full of sympathy and understanding for France. Time
worked on his side. Poincaré was defeated when
he went to the country for re-election, and contrary to nearly all the prophets, his policy was rejected and Herriot, corresponding to Ramsay Mac-
Donald as a leader of the Left, became Premier
of France.

THE UNCERTAIN PEACE

THE DEFEAT OF POINCARÉ

I was one of the few who had some inkling of the change of view in France and foretold the peril of Poincaré. In conversation with French people, and especially the ordinary working folk, I gathered that Poincaré no longer held their confidence. They had backed him when he ordered the occupation of the Ruhr, but only because they believed that he would "deliver the goods." Now they saw that the "goods" were not forthcoming, and that, instead of receiving large reparations from Germany, the franc was dropping, abruptly and perilously. They believed that M. Poincaré was a little too "rigid," too much of a lawyer, and too little of a business man. They were aware of all the hate that was being built up against them in Germany. They said—many of them—"We are afraid of the future."

It was above all that fear of the future, the terrifying spectre of a new war, when not the great Black Army of Africa, nor all their submarines, nor all their aeroplanes, would save France from another struggle in which the last of her youth would perish, which overthrew Poincaré and his

[175]

"rigid" methods. France, by a majority, desired peace, if that could be gained by some new policy, not surrendering security, not weak, but more in accord with the spirit of Liberalism.

There is no doubt in my mind that the result of the elections in Great Britain and the rise of Labour in that country had a powerful influence on the French election. It was a call back to democratic ideals in Europe, against the militarists and Imperialists.

Anyhow it gave Ramsay MacDonald a wonderful, an amazing chance. With Herriot, ex-Mayor of Lyons, advanced Liberal, leader of Labour in France, he could speak on equal terms. They understood each other's ideas. They knew each other's difficulties. Herriot, who speaks German well and has studied their system of civic organisation, had an honest desire to be fair and just to Germany while not betraying French interests. He did not call the German people *"Sales Boches."* He did not want to kill their babies or starve them to death. He acknowledged that they had a right to live. He wanted to deal with them on business terms and, if possible—if possible!—get their goodwill and free consent to a plan by which French

[176]

and Germans may live in the same world without periodical spasms of slaughter. With Herriot and Ramsay MacDonald in cordial agreement on the ideals of peace in the London Conference in August, ten years after the beginning of war, the peace of Europe had a greater chance than any other statesmen of England and France would have made conceivable. Luck, or Fate, was on the side of success.

THE LONDON AGREEMENT

Those meetings of the statesmen in No 10 Downing Street will make a dramatic chapter in history when they come to be written. Behind the representatives of each nation stood the forces of reaction; sullen, menacing, obstructive. Herriot knew that if he yielded too much he would be destroyed by the Conservatives of France, by that formidable power still held by Poincaré and all he stands for in French opinion. Marx and Streseman knew that if they surrendered too much they would be overwhelmed by a Nationalist outburst in their own country. Ramsay MacDonald knew that if he asked either side to ignore their

[177]

own public opinion the Conference would fail and
calamity would follow. The American Ambassador, Kellogg, knew that his people would refuse
to guarantee a loan to Germany unless France
withdrew demands which deprived it of all security. Time and time again the Conference was on
the point of breaking down. The international
bankers sat behind the scenes refusing to sanction
French plans for further penalties against Germany if she defaulted on future payments. There
was anguish among the Germans when Herriot
told them that his hands were tied regarding the
evacuation of the Ruhr and that no withdrawal
could be made until a year more had run. They
saw his difficulty as he saw theirs. The French
would unseat him if he conceded an earlier withdrawal. He pleaded with them to agree to this
condition—utterly opposed to the spirit of the
Dawes Report—for the sake of the loan of forty
million pounds sterling, future liberty, world
peace. The wires were hot with messages to and
from Berlin and Paris where the Governments insisted on national demands. The fate of Europe
trembled in the balance, until at last the German
representatives yielded to that year in the Ruhr,

under protest, with misgivings and forebodings, but with a hope that the enormous disappointment to the German people would be outweighed by the saving of their economic life, the future liberation from hostile occupation, a postponement, at least, of ruin. So the Dawes Report was accepted and signed, and the London Agreement began a new chapter of history in which there is a promise —another chance—of peace at last, and a spirit of conciliation between the nations.

PART III: THE PRESENT PERILS

PART III: THE PRESENT PERILS

THERE are still many danger zones through which our civilisation must pass before there is anything like security against calamities which might destroy it for a long chapter of history. There are still many points of peril which make one anxious even for the immediate future, and it seems to me that, without raising imaginary bogies or allowing pessimism to paint too dark a picture, it is necessary to look at these possible causes of trouble and to realise the very thin ground upon which we are all walking above smouldering fires.

The present dangers which must be eliminated somehow lest we all stagger on to catastrophe are of three kinds: racial, social, and economic. The last indeed is of such overwhelming influence upon racial rivalries and social upheavals that many students of modern history are inclined to believe that it is the underlying meaning of all wars, revolutions, and human struggles. The pressure of population, the need of food, the desire to get raw material for industrial manufactures, national competition to capture trade markets are, according to the modern school of thought, the main causes of international friction and explosive episodes.

I agree as to the terrific importance of economic facts, especially in this present time of history, when the world has been industrialised, but there are other instincts in the human heart beyond the need of food, other passions besides trade rivalry. The passion of race is one of them. The passion of liberty for the race or nation is intense. National pride, sentiment expressed in symbols, such as the Flag, religious fanaticism, such as that of Islam, set human hearts on fire and make them careless even of self-interest or self-preservation. Before looking at the economic struggle which is looming ahead, and in my opinion is going to be a possible cause of another world conflict, one may see signs of racial passion stirring in many parts of the world and threatening its future peace.

RACIAL PASSIONS

It is in the very heart of Europe. Certainly the majority of the German people refuse stubbornly to accept the consequences of the defeat inflicted upon them as more than a temporary check to their strength and supremacy among civilised people. They are so conscious of their own genius in organisation and industry, so confident in the future destiny of the German folk, so sure that their increasing population is bound to prevail over the weaker and dwindling stock of a nation like France, that they are only waiting for the time when, as they think, the inevitable laws of history will carry them in a tide over the present barriers that have been imposed upon them. Meanwhile, they rage at the humiliations they have to suffer, and brood over the injustice of their present condition. Their sense of being the victims of world injustice is a fixed idea or what, in the present jargon of psychoanalysis, is called a "complex." It is not less dangerous for that, and to regain their liberty of action, freedom from foreign interference with foreign occupation, and release from immense burdens of foreign debt, there are large numbers of Germans who would willingly die with a racial patriotism and passion exalted above all self-interest. Many old women in Germany would like to march with sharpened scissors behind the Ger-

[185]

man troops. Many young girls would gladly go with their hatpins to stab a Frenchman or two in revenge for the Ruhr. Europe will not be safe until that racial hatred between France and Germany has died down or has been killed by a new spirit and a community of interests. Herriot, the democratic Prime Minister of France, was the first to offer a truce to that hatred, and the new spirit has begun to work a little on both sides of the Rhine, though it is a delicate growth which will need great encouragement. In Hungary, and to a less extent in Austria, racial passion is also smouldering, and could be quickly fanned into flame. The Hungarians are a proud fighting race, who feel themselves superior to neighbours like the Serbs and Roumanians occupying some of their ancient territory. "It will not always be like this," some of them told me. "Something will break, and we shall move. Not all the tears of women will put out the red flame of that future war of liberation when we shall join hands with our kinsfolk and smash these artificial boundaries imposed by a scandalous peace."

The Balkans are still a stewpot of racial passions and rivalries—Serbs, Bulgars, Montenegrins,

[186]

Albanians, Roumanians, Greeks and Turks all snarling at each other, all waiting until the Great Powers get to grips again, or are too busy to intervene between these smaller nations.

THE RACIAL AMBITIONS OF RUSSIA

Russia is becoming race-conscious again. Now that the revolutionary period seems to have ended, and internal peace has been established, the Soviet Government is thinking far more racially than communistically. Communism no longer exists in Russia as a strict system. It died before Lenin, who re-established the right of private trading and private property with certain reservations which do not affect the private citizens within the state to any appreciable extent.

The Communistic propaganda is reserved mainly for foreign consumption, in order to create trouble in other states and especially to weaken those countries which are most antagonistic to the Russian form of government. Men like Radek and Tchicherin, whom I interviewed in Moscow at the time of famine, were beginning to think again of Russia as a world power. All their talk was of

[187]

that. They are Russians before they are Communists. They would be glad to see a world revolution, and their agents are doing what they can to provoke it, but mainly because they see the Slav race rising above that economic ruin and taking advantage of its weakness. Their eyes are turned to Riga, outside their present boundaries, as an open port when Petrograd is blocked by ice. They have no love for those new Baltic nations—Latvia, Esthonia, and Lithuania—which gained their independence at the expense of Russia. They hate the Poles, and the new war, if it happens in Europe, will begin when Germany and Russia try to join hands across the prostrate body of Poland.

The Germans are already in close commercial alliance with Russia. German ploughs, railway engines, manufactured goods, are being exchanged for Russian wheat, flax, furs, oil, and diamonds. The Russians do not love the Germans, but they will co-operate with them in self-interest. A German revolution would please them mightily. But German Imperialism will not be spurned by Soviet Russia, certainly not by Tchicherin and his friends, if a military and trade alliance would re-

[188]

sult in the downfall of Poland, followed perhaps by the capture of Constantinople and the way through Serbia to the Adriatic.

The old dreams of Pan-Slavism are stirring again among those who control the destiny of Russia. Radek, the chief propagandist, sees red in the direction of India and Afghanistan. The downfall of the British "Raj" in India might be followed by a Russian Empire in the East.

THE DARK HORSE

Russia is the Dark Horse of Europe. It is impossible to foretell what road it will travel. Above the mass of ignorant and patient peasants, desiring peace in their fields and praying God for good harvests, there is a crowd of nimble-minded men holding the machinery of power; ambitious, cynical, with some cause, of the high moralities preached by other powers, unscrupulous and adventurous. Some of them, in my opinion most of them, are not personally ambitious for gold or luxury or greed. They lead austere lives. Tchicherin spends most of his days and nights in two little rooms barely furnished. Radek has an

[189]

untidy old den crammed with books along a white-washed corridor in the Kremlin. Most of them, I believe, have a sincere desire to improve the conditions of their people, to eliminate disease, to give them a decent share of human happiness. They were relentless against their political enemies, like all leaders of revolution who live in terror of re-action, and by their terror are made cruel. They have an Oriental indifference for human life, and they believe that a life is forfeited by crime or political hostility to their way of rule. Many of these men were not personally responsible for the atrocities which happened in the fever and fright-fulness of revolutionary madness. They are intellectual, highly educated, irreligious men, devoid of sentiment, suspicious of each other, with a cold passionate hatred for the old régime, and with a fanatical belief in their own form of tyranny, a contempt for the ignorance of the peasant mind, and a detestation of the Orthodox Church and all forms of Christian faith, as many of the recent Ministers of France, including Clemenceau, Mille-rand and Briand were in earlier days. They are amused by the fear of "Bolshevism" in other countries. It flatters their vanity and appeals to their sense of humour. Many are for the most part "realists" who believe in Force as the only argument, or, failing force, guile. They are not, as a class, pacifists or humanitarians, nor do they trouble to give any lip service to their ideals. In the Red Army, officered by many sons of the old *bourgeoisie,* they have a weapon which is not negligible in training or equipment. As ambassadors and agents they have men whose intellectual abilities are more than a match for the elder statesmen of Europe and not bound by the same code of honour because the foundations of their faith are different. Many of their officials and agents are honest and patriotic men, desiring to serve their people in a time of dreadful uncertainty, and all over Russia there are men and women—millions of them—who accept the Soviet Government as something better than Tsardom, however bad, and, while hostile or scornful secretly to the "eyewash" of Soviet propaganda, give their labour ungrudgingly for the sake of Russia and the reconstruction of its life after war and revolution. They believe in peace, but many would fight for Russian liberty against Royalist invaders. They even give the Soviet Government the credit of good inten-

[191]

tion towards the people, and believe in the "idealism" of Lenin and the "genius" of Trotsky, and the patriotism of other men who in the outside world are painted as devils incarnate.

THE RUSSIAN FOLK

It is false to think that the majority of the Russian people are living in a state of sullen subjection under a hated tyranny. There are many who think so and suffer the agony of despair. But as far as I could see and learn the ordinary mass of people, peasants, artisans, and the Soviet workers, do not trouble about politics, and dislike the Government and its petty laws and restrictions neither more nor less than most primitive peoples dislike the far-off power that imposes taxes, issues disagreeable by-laws and regulations, and makes a mess of things from their point of view. Far from Moscow and its Soviets the village folk in Russia carry on much as they did under Tsardom, with more land, less flogging, the same amount of lice and periodical famine. Moscow may say: "Religion is the opium of the people," but the Russian peasants cross themselves before their ikons and pray God for daily bread. The *"Pravda"* may publish many lies about England or the United States, and prophesy world revolution once a week, but not many of the hundred million Russian peasants ever read the *"Pravda."* They sow their seed, plough and reap, scrape a hard life out of the earth, love their children, beat their wives at times, die in great numbers with Oriental resignation to the Will of God in times of famine and disease.

Greater than the little ruthless men in Moscow, or the fanatics there, or the idealists, or the atheistic "intellectuals" is the life in the fields of Russia with its obedience to the laws of nature—very cruel sometimes—its family love, its faith, its superstition, its dignity, labour, courage, simplicity, and ordinary human passions. The danger to Europe and the world is the control of Russian manhood by a small group whose orders must be obeyed because they hold the power of life and death and in any case are the leaders of the Russian race for weal or woe, in peace or war.

Ramsay MacDonald's attempt to formulate a Treaty with the Soviet states of Russia was, I believe, inspired by the hope that the official recognition of that form of government would lead to its modification on more liberal lines and to trade relations by which a hundred million people might be brought back to the commonwealth of Europe. It was also no doubt a sop to the extremists behind his own party who have a sentimental sympathy with the Russian revolution and believe that Communism, whatever its failure in Russia, is the ideal towards which humanity should strive.

I agree with Ramsay MacDonald and his followers that it is fantastic to expect the repayment of the Russian war debt, amounting to £1,000,000,-000 to Great Britain alone, and that instead of keeping these mythical figures in the national account book they may as well be wiped out as a bad debt belonging to a bad past. But Mr. Ramsay MacDonald, honest as he is in many ways, was deceiving himself and his followers, as well as the Russian people, when he promised them the possibility of a great loan. There is no possibility of any such loan, first, because England cannot spare the capital, and, second, because Russia offers no security which would be accepted by business men. While the Russian leaders are still encouraging world revolution, fermenting social strife in many countries, and declaring war on capital outside their own frontiers, it is idle to think that English capitalists will entrust their money to the Russian government. It would be like fond parents throwing their babes to the wolves at the amiable suggestion of the village idiot. The hostility of the Liberals and Conservatives was so united against the proposal of a guaranteed loan to Russia that Ramsay MacDonald and his Labour government were faced with certain defeat. This was only accelerated by a few days when the Labour government fell, on October 8th of this year, on a vote of censure for withdrawing a prosecution against a Communist writer for a seditious article inspired by the Red propaganda of Moscow.

Although in my opinion the guarantee of a loan to Russia is not within the bounds of business common sense so long as the Soviet Government refuses to obey the usual moralities of international relations, I am convinced that England and other countries will be ill advised if they refuse to "recognise" the present rulers of Russia—recognition not meaning approval—or to encourage trade relations with them independent of national loans.

[195]

As long as Russia is isolated and ostracised the Soviet tyranny will be maintained, a great potential market will be closed to the world, and Red propaganda will work in an underground way to promote revolution in Europe and Asia. But with recognition, which means diplomatic intercourse, the enterprise of private traders, and the admission of Russia to the League of Nations, the Russian people would be brought back to the family of nations, and it is possible, even likely, that their present rulers would be influenced, modified and liberalised by the general pressure of world opinion. What Russia needs as a moral cure is the fresh air of international intercourse.

THE CLASH OF COLOUR

There is a new peril in the world which is already becoming a bogey in the imagination of men. It is the "Rising Tide of Colour." I do not believe in a world conspiracy of the coloured races to overthrow white rule. I do not believe in a new challenge of the Mohammedan peoples to Christendom. But I do believe that the massacre of the World War and some of its lessons and watchwords have aroused passions and ambitions among the dark-skinned races which will lead to many new problems and perils. The British Empire is face to face with these in India, Egypt and Asia. France, Italy and Spain will have to face them in Northern Africa. America will have to face them in her own southern states and on the Pacific coast. That ringing phrase, "the self-determination of peoples," was translated into many tongues East as well as West. "A War for Liberty" was an ideal which was carried across the deserts and into the very jungles of the world. Young Indian students at Oxford or Cambridge or London University saw the war fever in Europe, read its rhetoric, thrilled to the words of President Wilson, saw the weakening of European power, the overthrow of dynasties, the setting up of new nations, the proclamation of independence for Poland, Ireland, Czecho-Slovakia, all sorts of states and races, the triumph of Turkey in Asia Minor. They asked themselves a whispered question: "How about India?" The young Egyptians said: "How about Egypt?" The Arab race said: "Independence is good for us as well as for others." The overthrow of "tyrannies" is very catching, even though one form of tyranny is substituted for another. The spirit of revolt travels far and is infectious, especially when it is carried by home-going soldiers who have fought in other people's wars, as Indian troops in Palestine, Mesopotamia, and, for a time, against their will, in France.

INDIA, EGYPT, AFRICA

The British people are already confronted with grave troubles in India and Egypt and the Soudan. History has placed responsibilities on their shoulder which they cannot shrug off with a careless gesture of indifference or a splendid gesture of renunciation. That welter of races and religions in India cannot be abandoned by people who have ruled it, given it law, justice, internal peace, and protection from old cruelties, tyrannies, famine and disease. If the British lost their hold on India there would be a world of anarchy among all those races and creeds between which there is no tolerance, so that they cannot eat together, or mingle in a crowd, or touch without defilement. If the British lost India other powers would fight to take it and the world would be aflame again.

[198]

THE PRESENT PERILS

England will lose India if she grants self-government too quickly, or too generously, to native rulers who cannot hold the scales of justice, even as England has held them; who cannot control the native princes by any such allegiance as they have given to a white emperor; who could not keep Hindus and Moslems and other religious fanatics from each other's throats, nor administer justice with common sense and impartial judgment, as young magistrates from English public schools in remote districts, where they were law-makers, judges, administrators, in the midst of native populations obedient to their verdict and with faith in their honesty. But the agitators in India, the "holy men" like Ghandi, the students with Western education are in revolt against this benevolent despotism. They believe that India is able to govern itself. They are refusing to buy British-made goods. They use "Liberty" as their watchword, and those who believe in national liberty, as I do, can only answer their arguments by saying that India is not a nation but a collection of races, and that Western ideas of parliamentary government, "no taxation without representation" cannot be translated into an Oriental country before centuries of education and preparation, nor—failing that—without an anarchy in which a thousand horrors would happen. To the fanatical Indian student from King's College, London, that answer is taken as an insult and as hypocrisy. And yet it is true.

So also in Egypt and the Soudan. The Egyptians ignore the benefits that have come to them from British rule, British engineering, British science, which dammed the Nile and fertilised their fields, gave a better chance of life to the peasants, brought peace from the passions, barbarities, slave-driving of the African races. They have a new sense of power because they know England's need of peace. They are prepared to blot out all British benefits for the sake of that cry, "Egypt for the Egyptians!" shouted from Cairo across the deserts. They demand the Soudan as their province, although it was subdued by British troops and its barbarism was tamed by British rule after a history of human cruelty in this black region hellish in its torture and diabolism, to which beyond any doubt, it will return if by weakness of man power, hatred of war, or economic poverty, the British government releases its control.

England is the leader of world peace. Poverty

[200]

is creeping closer to her. Her old Imperial spirit is deadened by war weariness and by new ideals of liberal policy from which military force is eliminated. Yet by their Imperial heritage the British people have responsibilities towards the coloured races which cannot be supported without force of arms, as military police for the order of the human race. If Great Britain, for reasons of economy or lack of strength, retires from these regions, as the Romans did from their own wide Empire, chaos and upheavals in Africa, India and Asia will let loose a world of human passion and revolt. Other powers will claim the succession, and another world war, on a more terrible scale, will begin.

THE FRENCH IN MOROCCO

France is storing up trouble for herself in North Africa by raising her Colonial Army from the dark-skinned races. She is training Arabs and negroes to handle machine-guns with great efficiency, to throw the latest type of bombs, to be familiar with field guns and heavy artillery, to shoot straight with the rifle and stab straight with the bayonet.

The French military leaders are justly proud of

their work in Morocco. Marshal Lyautey under-
stands the Arab mind as no other man. The
French colonial officers have a wonderful skill and
sympathy with the legions under their command.
But can France be sure that this army they have
created will be loyal to French interests, and will
fight eagerly, even gladly, against German shell-
fire and poison-gas if ever France is again attacked
by the same enemy? In the last war the coloured
troops were sacrificed in many battles. They were
led like sheep to the shambles, or rather like tigers
to the pits of death. They did not like it. Those
who escaped the slaughter and went home told
frightful tales. Already there is a spirit of revolt
stirring in Morocco below the surface of loyalty to
France. Some of the Arab tribes in French Morocco are joining hands with those fighting against
Spain. "Our time is coming," said an Arab guide
to a recent traveller. "We shall sweep the *Feringhi*
into the sea—like that!" He made an arrogant
gesture and smiled, with ferocity in his eyes.
France will have trouble with her Colonial troops,
and it will be a dirty business in future history.

Those are some of the danger zones of our
present state; and I have said nothing about Japan

or China, in which there is no standing still in the Oriental quietude of ancient history. Japan has learnt to use modern weapons on sea and land. She has great ambitions. The white races have got to be careful lest they are weakened and exhausted by wars of their own, and let their own causes of quarrel blind them and make them mad.

THE ECONOMIC STRUGGLE

Meanwhile the economic struggle between the white nations is threatening to develop with a severity of competition which is alarming to all students of international affairs. Great Britain and the United States of America are bound to be competitors in the world market against nations able to produce manufactured articles at far less cost owing to cheap labour. The United States will undoubtedly make a serious effort to overcome this difficulty by cutting into the international trade with surplus products on a small margin of profit, but whether they succeed or not does not matter very much to the life and prosperity of their people, who are self-supporting and self-contained. For Great Britain it is literally a matter of life and

[203]

death as a great power. To feed their population England, Scotland and Wales have to import more than nine months' food supplies, which can only be paid for by the export of raw material and manufactured goods. In the same way they must pay for the essential services of the nation, including the Army, Navy, and Civil Service. At the present time Great Britain has succeeded in regaining her export trade to over seventy per cent. of its prewar standard of money values; but that is not nearly enough now that her population, ten years after, has increased by nearly two millions, and now that the cost of life and production is very much higher than in 1913 owing to the burden of taxation, the higher rate of wages, and the lower purchasing power of English money.

There is no certainty that Great Britain will be able to maintain her present standard of export trade, apart altogether from increasing it. In various classes of goods, in which for half a century the British people had something like a monopoly in foreign markets, there is no longer that advantage. India is boycotting cotton fabric made in Lancashire and has her own mills hard at work. Italy is producing cotton goods at much lower prices than she could formerly buy them in England, owing to the development of water power which relieves her of the price of British coal—a severe loss to the Welsh coalfields—and cheap labour. In steel and iron England is losing her supremacy. Germany and France separately have eaten into this big industry. Together, by a working arrangement between the Ruhr and Lorraine, they will put up a combination of power which may deal a knock-out blow to British steel works. Already, owing to the cheapness of German contracts, many British blast furnaces are closing down and the ugly notice is going up: "No hands wanted." It is discouraging to read the statistics of British trade each month recording "stagnation" or "quietude" or "a gloomy outlook" in many great industries. It is alarming to an Englishman to have a vision of future years when conditions may be worse than this owing to the conditions of labour in competing nations.

THE PRICE OF LABOUR

The price of labour is at the root of the problem. Even before the war the rate of wages in England, as calculated in purchasing power, were far higher than in Germany, Belgium, Italy, France, and most other continental nations, though very much less than in the United States. During the war Labour, seeing its chance, demanded fantastic rates of pay and received them. During the last two years there has been a readjustment to the cost of living so that wages have been reduced, but they still stand in nearly all trades, except that of agriculture, at a higher level than in 1913.

But the men are not satisfied. During the war they learnt their power and their value. Since the war they have become intensely class-conscious and demand better wages, shorter hours, decent conditions of housing, security in sickness and un-employment, old-age pensions from sixty years on, more money to be spent on their education, and a bigger margin beyond the bare needs of life for leisure and amusement. I am not one of those who blame them. I am all—or nearly all—on their side. The conditions of the slums in England and Scotland are still a disgrace to civilisation. The housing accommodation of working men in villages as well as in cities is often abominable. I do not believe in a great Empire or a luxurious civilisation

[206]

built on the wreckage of men's lives, or slave labour, on the killing of souls, as the British Empire
was built during the industrial period after the
Napoleonic Wars, when the manufacturers of
Great Britain grew rich out of sweated labour in
factories and homes before the Trades Unions, the
Factory Acts, and democratic reform blotted out
the black shame of 1830 to 1850. I think it good
and right that men who help to save their country
should be given the reward of good wages for good
work and some chance of joy in life. The point of
trouble is not the justice of that but its possibility.
Is it possible for these labouring classes in England,
Scotland, and Wales to get high wages and work
for shorter hours when their export trade is diminishing, when the competition of cheap labour will
become more and more severe during the next few
years, and when the taxation of the wealthy classes
is already extinguishing their wealth?

Labour in the mass, especially the political extremists who accuse Ramsay MacDonald of being
a "bourgeois" and Philip Snowden a "reactionary," believe that it is possible. They believe that
there is still a vast source of untapped wealth in
England which should be redistributed in their

[207]

favour. They believe that they would get far
higher wages and work much less if they owned and
controlled the machinery and material of labour
by some system of nationalisation or communism.
They believe that it is only the selfishness of the
"upper classes" and the greed of the great employ-
ers and Trusts which prevent them from receiving
far greater rewards in return for their toil. They
have not yet realised, or refuse to believe, that
England is not in possession of inexhaustible
wealth, that the rich people in the country—with
only few exceptions—are already taxed beyond
their power to pay without crippling industry itself
and slowing down the adventure of trade, and that
if a nation loses its markets for the only goods it
can produce no amount of social legislation or social
revolution will benefit the individual.

The awful failure of the Russian Communism,
its abandonment by its own leaders, is either unknown or ignored by many British working men.
Some of them would like to try the experiment in
Great Britain. They do not understand the extreme delicacy of that machinery of international
trade and credit by which the industrial life of
Great Britain has been maintained. Russia lost

[208]

its international trade, but its life was secure from the soil, apart from drought. All factories might close down in Petrograd, as they did, but the workers returned to the land and scraped along. In Great Britain if the factories close for lack of markets or credit or capital, the population will surely die unless America comes to the rescue with the A.R.A.

I don't think it will be as bad as that. Before such things could happen madness would have to overtake the British people and they are, as a nation, remarkably sane. Communism is not a spreading disease in the heart of England, though it lurks in cities where trade is worst. But even with full sanity, the moderation of such a Labour Government as that led by Ramsay MacDonald, and a gradual redistribution of wealth already taking place, there is bound to be trouble ahead. In my judgment England must steel herself to endure lean years, heavier burdens, fiercer competition, less luxury all around, harder work for less pay.

GERMAN COMPETITION

It is uncertain yet whether the London Agreement embodying the Dawes Report will actually be fulfilled by Germany. In my belief it will not be fulfilled. It is impossible for me to believe that Germany is capable of paying a hundred and twenty-five million pounds sterling and more in a rising scale for an indefinite number of years. England could not do so, and England is richer than Germany. The American debt, which is being paid off at the rate of £35,000,000 a year, is a burden which makes Great Britain breathe hard. That is hardly more than one quarter of what the German people are expected to pay, and I do not think they can do so for more than a few years. They can only do so, as I have pointed out, in one way: by creating a trade balance in their favour which would enable them to transfer that sum to their creditors after paying for the essential services of their own nation. If they are able to get such a trade balance it will mean that they are overwhelming the world markets with German goods. Who is going to let them do so? The United States would surely put up barriers against their manufactured articles.

[210]

Great Britain will not admit them in such an over-powering quantity, whatever her theoretical allegiance to Free Trade. In other markets these cheap German goods will oust British and American competitors. The factories of Great Britain will be producing articles at a price which other nations will refuse to pay when Germany is canvassing for contracts. Germany will default again, I am certain, unless by a miracle of industry her people, on slave wages, capture the world's trade, which would be worse than default to British manufacturers and in a less degree to those in America.

Whatever happens it is a serious outlook, because default would mean a new political crisis in Europe—all the old wounds open again—and success would ruin those who have imposed the Agreement. The horns of that dilemma were seen years ago by M. Loucheur, the greatest expert of economics in France. Speaking before the Senate he said: "Germany cannot pay these indemnities. If she were able to pay it would make her master of the world's trade. Let us therefore insist on security rather than on reparations."

The revival of Germany, limited by these enormous reparations, will undoubtedly increase the

[211]

general prosperity of all European nations. The restoration of German purchasing power by a loan of £40,000,000 from Great Britain and the United States, stabilising her monetary system, will help world trade everywhere to the extent that Germany buys raw material for her industries and additional luxuries and comforts in foreign countries. Australia and Canada will benefit by purchases of wool and meat. They will buy more from the Mother Country in consequence. Holland, Denmark, Sweden, Italy and France will exchange more products. The wheel of world trade will turn more rapidly. Great Britain and the United States will find Germany a better customer. But Great Britain will also find Germany a stronger competitor, and the advantages which may come to the British people by the recovery of prosperity in Europe may be outweighed by that competition owing to the difference between dear labour and cheap labour. Already, ten years after the beginning of the war, Germany is able to offer steel to Middlesbrough at thirty shillings a ton less than it costs to manufacture steel in Middlesbrough itself! I have the greatest sympathy with organised labour in England which is endeavouring to maintain its standard

[212]

of life and wages and even to improve them. But
the socialists who are legislating for shorter hours,
more pay, larger doles for unemployed, national
subsidies in the building trade, and national money
for providing work, are up against the industry of
German labour which is working nine and ten
hours a day, instead of the eight hours in England,
at less than half the rate of pay. In great industrial
cities like Sheffield something like a third of the
working population is living on charity or the
official dole. It is impossible for a nation to maintain its economic life on such a tragic basis. It
must be put upon sounder foundations or come
down with a crash.

ILLUSIONS OF THE SOCIALISTS

The peril in England at the present time is the
illusion of political leaders in the Socialist Party
that the prosperity of the working classes may be
increased without any regard to the economic conditions in other countries. The painful truth is
that these conditions of cheap labour and long
hours, better organisation and greater mechanical
skill, will come smashing into the dreams of the

[213]

social idealists with heavy blows of abominable reality.

I do not believe that in our time Great Britain will regain the old standards of her world trade. It is my firm belief that the next period of history will see a slowing down in the international exchange of manufactured goods, and that most countries will have to restrict their imports because their exports are not wanted on the same scale. That is to say the nations will become more self-contained, relying more than ever upon their own supplies of food and the internal exchange of their own industries. The English people must get back to agriculture, instead of relying almost exclusively on manufactures and buying most of their food abroad, and large numbers of their overcrowded populations in the great cities must get back to the fields at home, or in the Dominions, where there is room for all. Otherwise they will surely perish in pauperdom.

Before that happens there is bound to be political strife and social unrest on a serious and perilous scale. Not only in Great Britain but all over the world, the intensity of this new competition, the gravity of this readjustment to new and restricted conditions of economic life, will provide an excuse for agitators and revolutionaries who desire to overthrow the whole structure of our present system of Capital and Labour in the hope of obtaining greater prosperity for the labouring folk and a broader control of the sources of wealth. Communism, defeated in Russia, will seek victories in other countries more highly organised, and the Fascisti, who are in all countries under different names, will seek to protect their property, privileges and principles by violent action against this challenge. The bitterness and the need of nations threatened with economic poverty, unable to support their industrial populations, thwarted in their attempt to enlarge their boundaries, will lead to new international jealousies which will tempt their militarists and their hot-heads to risk again the adventure of war. The spectre of revolution has not been exorcised from Europe, and all these pressures of populations, passions, trade interests, industrial rivalries, and social ambitions are full of explosive forces which may lead to another world conflict, unless there is a new vision at work in the heart of humanity. It is all very difficult!

PART IV: THE HOPE AHEAD

PART IV: THE HOPE AHEAD

IT seems like pessimism to deal so much with
the difficulties and dangers of our present state.
But one would be guilty of cowardice if one's mind
shirked these unpleasant facts, and of extreme folly
if one pretended to oneself that peace and prosperity are bound to come. They will only come if
the evil forces that are active beneath our present
uncertain peace and in the minds of men in many
groups are checked, if not killed, by increasing
knowledge, by counsels of international goodwill,
by a spiritual revolt against the dark powers among
masses of the common folk, and by wise and noble
leadership.

In spite of all that I have put down on the black
side of the picture, I am optimistic enough to believe, or at least to hope, that good may possibly
prevail over ill will, that knowledge and wisdom
are beginning to tell, just a little, against ignorance
and insanity, and that after the frightful lessons
of the last ten years a majority of people in many

countries are eager to find some settlement of old causes of quarrels, old hatreds, new hostilities and future conflict, by friendly compromise and good statesmanship. That, after all, is a very great hope indeed. If we have moved as far as that, and I think we have, we are some way along the road to a better kind of world.

Not all the goodwill in the world will cure some of the troubles to which I have alluded. It will not eliminate the competition between cheap labour and dear labour. It will not restore the wealth wasted in the war nor the youth that died with splendid quality of blood and spirit. It will not relieve the pressure of enormous populations seeking, and not finding, their old markets or new fields of trade. Not quickly, anyhow. But knowledge and goodwill, a higher sense of spiritual values, and a determination to limit the areas and occasions of conflict, will at least ease the burdens and anxieties of mankind, and prevent another world war, or a series of spasmodic wars, until in a more distant future folly and force or some natural irresistible struggle for existence may play the devil again.

THE HOPE AHEAD

THE SPIRIT OF PEACE

There are many hopeful signs in the world to-day which counteract the evil elements. The peace spirit is spreading between nations, if not between classes. The British people, in the Mother Country and in the sister nations of the Empire, stand solidly and almost passionately for peace in the world. It is true, as cynics point out, that the material interests of the British Empire are safe-guarded by peace, and that poverty in gold and man-power and military strength has brought about this dove-like attitude. That is true, but not all the truth, nor the best part of it.

It is also true that in most of the homes in England, Scotland and Wales the memory of dead boys sacrificed to the war spirit has produced a loathing of war which compels these people to seek for some new leadership, some new philosophy of states-manship, some new system of international agree-ment, which will prevent another sacrifice like that among their children and children's children. They may not regret with passionate revolt the call which caused those boys of ours to die—though many do—and they may believe with unchanging faith that

[221]

if it happened again in that way the duty of youth would be to fight as they fought and die as they died in a righteous cause and in defence of that country. There are not many pacifists in England or Scotland who think that all war is wrong, or even that the last war was wrong. But they are all pacifists in believing that another war must be prevented by eliminating the causes of quarrel. They are all League of Nations men—and women—in allegiance to the spirit of the League, even if they deplore its weakness and futility. In the vast majority they would refuse now to follow any leadership which involved them in war, beyond military police work on far frontiers, unless the safety of the Empire or civilisation itself were utterly at stake.

That may seem like "hedging." It leaves a loophole for wars in India, Africa, Egypt. To some extent it is "hedging," for even the Labour Party, most vowed to peace, is prepared to use the regular army for the protection of the Soudan or the crushing of rebellion in India. But with certain mental reservations and irresistible exceptions, which I think all nations would make (the greatest pacifists in the United States would advocate force against

[222]

a Black rebellion in the Southern States), the British people, apart from a very small minority, will give an eager support to any plan for general disarmament down to the irreducible minimum for maintaining the military police work of the world, and will be hostile to any power or leadership which is convicted of warlike policy and designs. It is not a negligible fact in world history when an assembly of nations like the British Empire is dedicated to the spirit of international peace, at least within the confines of the white races of the world, and, if possible, of liberal forms of government, gradual relaxation of direct control in its Eastern world. It is the first time that it has happened with such spiritual conviction in the minds of millions.

THE AMERICAN SLOGAN FOR PEACE

The United States is also pacific in purpose and in spirit. The American people have already in some ways taken up the leadership in the plan of peace. It was Mr. Secretary Hughes who carried through the Washington Agreement for naval disarmament and suggested the calling of the Dawes

[223]

Committee. There is no doubt that the American Government will throw its weight of influence on behalf of a reasonable scheme for the general disarmament. It is, however, by the efforts of individuals and societies in the United States that public opinion in that country is being educated in the ideals of international peace. A great tide of pacifist emotion is beating up from the women's clubs and all that vast number of idealistic groups which find expression in Summer Schools, Chatauqua lectures, literary societies, and political institutions which form a highly organised system of propaganda and "uplift" throughout the States by which mass opinion is formed and stimulated.

One can hardly exaggerate the power of this educative force in the minds of a hundred and ten million peoples. In no other country in the world is there such means of swaying public opinion towards a single ideal by emotional appeal. That is not without danger, because it might swing violently to some passionate impulse in response to some real or imaginary danger, challenge, or insult to the honour or interests of the American people. But at the present time they are "out" for world peace. Whatever administration is in power it will be subject to the pressure and insistence of a vast majority eager to subscribe to some plan which will demilitarise the civilised nations to a reasonable minimum of strength, and substitute international arbitration and law for the old argument and ordeal of battle, while maintaining the independence of the United States from all alliances and "entanglements." It seems to me a national policy, not only wise and justified in its reservations, but immensely helpful to the progress of the peace idea. A close alliance with the United States would be tempting to Great Britain and France. But in my opinion it would be a calamity, because it would create a new "Balance of Power" so formidable that the other nations of the earth would either have to obey its dictates, just or unjust, or resist it by force. It will be far better for the world if the United States remains an arbitrator, and does not become an ally of any group of powers.

THE OLD ENEMIES

The peace spirit which is pervading the mentality of the British Empire and the United States is beginning to work in the mind of individuals and

[225]

groups even among those Europeon peoples who are closest to the danger zone and most tempted by reactionary tendencies in favour of force for defence or vengeance.

Even in France, which is reasonably afraid of what may happen when Germany gets strong again, there is an increasing desire to obtain security by justice and conciliation rather than by military domination and a policy of coercion.

Even in Germany, resentful, bitter, brooding over "injustice," inflamed to dreams of vengeance by old and new leaders who believe only in force and hatred, there are groups of idealists, societies of youth, bodies of working men, who are putting up a spiritual resistance to their Junkers and Nationalists. In spite of all their military parades in Bavaria, their secret drillings, their harking back to the sentiment of the old Imperialism, their hatred of France—most dangerous, as I have said —millions of working men and women in Germany have a loathing of war (its horror is in their souls) which would make them revolt against any attempts to prepare for a war of vengeance. Those people— convinced pacifists—are, I think, in a minority. The French adventure in the Ruhr weakened and

almost destroyed, for the time, pacifist sentiment in
Germany by causing an outburst of fury which has
left smouldering fires of resentment and rage. But
some of that will pass if the London Agreement is
carried out by France in a generous spirit, and
especially if the Ruhr is evacuated before another
year has gone. It is my personal belief that the
Nationalists will not have general support in the
country for a revival of militarism if France relieves
the pressure on Germany and makes a working
agreement with her industrialists for their mutual
benefit.

If Germany asks for war again she will get revolution first.

LIBERAL THOUGHT IN FRANCE

The hope of Europe—one good hope at least—
is the new attitude of France under the Herriot
Government. In his great speech defending the
acceptance of the London Agreement it was signifi-
cant that loud cheers were raised when he said that
an end had been put to "the romantic idea that in
order to make certain of the fruits of victory Germany must be ruined." France, he said, must no

longer count only on force and ultimatums. At present she needed to rest, to restore her finances, to build up her population. "Reassure the mothers!" he cried, amidst passionate applause from the Left. "That also is patriotism." Those words to the mothers of France found an echo in the hearts of all those women who have lost their sons. France, above all, dreads a new sacrifice of youth, and the policy of Poincaré failed because it seemed to lead to that necessity, and aroused the fear of the peasant farmers and small shopkeepers who remember their dead sons.

The London Agreement, based on the Dawes Report, may break down in its financial operations. I believe it will, for the reasons I have given. But those words of Herriot renouncing the romantic idea of Germany's ruin as the fruits of victory for France promise a way of further compromise and conciliation if the burden of the London Agreement cannot be fulfilled, literally, by the German people, or if the effect of fulfilment is disastrous to other nations.

The London Agreement, after all, is only the first step towards the pacification of Europe, and its greatest benefit will be its clearing the way for other steps along the road to stable conditions and general security. The first of these is the de-militarisation of Europe, a relief from the crushing costs of great standing armies, preceded by absolute guarantees to prevent the re-arming of Germany. "The central fortress of Europe," said Herriot, "must be demolished, and the German democrats must aid us." That was a figure of rhetoric, for at the present time the "fortress" of Germany is dismantled of great artillery and under the power of French guns. But the French Premier was holding out a new hope for the world when he promised that France would base her security upon the moral guarantee of the world powers acting through the military control of Germany by the League of Nations in a general scheme of dis-armament.

One other Conference and attempt at settlement will arise out of the London Agreement. That is the question of inter-allied debts, overshadowing the financial relations of the world and the cause of grave anxiety and much antagonism. At the present time Great Britain is the only country paying off her war debts. In spite of payments to the United States, which are weighing heavily upon her

[229]

financial health, she is not receiving a penny from France or other countries to which she lent far more than she borrowed from the United States. If Germany is able to pay substantial reparations to France, Belgium and Great Britain, it will be an easy matter of arithmetic to write off many of these debts all round. I do not think it is going to be as easy as all this, because the future of German reparations is vastly uncertain. Nevertheless it is impossible for England to demand her "pound of flesh" from France if Germany is reprieved. I think England will act more generously than she can afford for the sake of goodwill all round, and I hope the United States will help her to be generous. . . .

If all that could be cleared away, Europe and the whole world would indeed be in possession of a fair field of hope in which we could sow and reap new harvests in the security of peace. There is bound to be much trouble, argument, friction, heart-burning, before that work is accomplished, yet we are moving slowly along to that endeavour, and there is a light in the sky beyond the jungle of all the undergrowth in which international relations are entangled.

[230]

THE HOPE AHEAD

THE MACHINERY OF DESTRUCTION

They are, after all, details. The spirit matters more than the letter. I think that in the spirit of the world, almost everywhere, there is a growing consciousness that the perils of new conflict are so frightful that civilisation might actually go down in chaos if the forces of evil are not subdued. At the back of many minds is the awful thought that machinery threatens to become the master of men and that science threatens to destroy humanity unless it is controlled. What were human valour, spiritual courage, superb physique, in the last war, up against long-range guns, aerial torpedoes, high explosives in concentrated fire, poison gas? At a distance of forty miles a platoon of men might be wiped out by a casual shell loosed from a fifteen-inch howitzer. What was the value of discipline, ardour, human strength, centuries of character building, to produce the fine flower of civilisation in the face of that explosive force which tore men's bodies to bits far from the sight of their enemy, without means of resistance on their part, with no more defence than if a thunderbolt had struck them? That is not war between human forces. It

[231]

is war with engines constructed by men but over-powering. Or, of what use were fair physique, athletic youth, soldierly qualities, heroic human stuff, when suddenly they were enveloped in a vapour which choked them, burnt their lungs, blinded them, stupefied them? All the discoveries of science which made men proud of the knowledge they had wrested from nature's most hidden secrets, like gods, were used for this devilish purpose of in-creasing the efficiency of human slaughter. Even the victory of flight which had baffled humanity since men first walked on earth and envied the birds for their liberty of the sky was achieved in time to increase the terrors and range of war.

Yet we know that if there is a next war it will be worse than the last because the poison gases are more deadly, the guns have longer range, the aero-planes will be more crowded in the sky, the cities will be more at the mercy of falling bombs. In many laboratories scientists are searching for new forms of destruction which may even make those weapons obsolete because so limited in their power of slaughter. It is not only possible but likely that some "death ray" projecting wireless force may sweep a countryside with a heat that would turn everything to flame and then to dust and ashes. Is mankind going to risk such an infernal ending to all its dreams of beauty and order and more perfect life? Is it going to allow its stupid brawls, its national ambitions, its little points of honour and argument, to be settled by this latest type of warfare which does not spare women or children, but, indeed, makes them the victims of its worst cruelties? With all its passionate follies, humanity can hardly be as mad as that.

THE REVOLT AGAINST WAR

I believe that before it is likely to happen the common folk of all countries will revolt from such a method of argument and demand some other means of settlement. The memory of the last war endures among those who realised its agony. Its futility is understood even by those who directed its forces. In Great Britain the generals—or many of them—are most convinced of the need of peace. In France Marshal Foch and many of those who led France to a victory at frightful cost wish to avoid another conflict beyond any other consideration. Some of them may believe in a supreme army as the only defence of peace, but it is peace and security which dominate their minds, not military adventures for ambition's sake. In Canada, Australia, and New Zealand the Generals of the Dominion forces are peace propagandists. In the United States the commanding officers who went to France are most in favour of generosity to Germany, within the limits of justice.

"What have we gained by the World War?" asked *The American Legion Weekly* ten years after that war began. The answers came from many great people and with few exceptions they saw more loss than gain, and in most cases all loss and no gain. I was most struck by the answer of General Sir Arthur Currie, who commanded the Canadians many times in great battles. I met him often and prophesied his military genius. His strength of character, his stubborn will power, his clear-cut judgment, marked him out as a man of great generalship and his record proved it, I think. He was not popular with his men. They thought him ruthless. He was ruthless, while the war went on, but this was his message to the American Legion, founded to perpetuate the memories of the war, and rather prone, it was thought, for a time, to perpetuate the memories of hate and the use of force.

"By the World War we gained a truer appreciation and a better realisation of war's unspeakable waste, its dreadful hardships, its cruel slaughter, and its aftermath of loneliness, sorrow and broken hearts. We now know that, as a means of solving the world's problems and removing international discord, war is a delusion and a lie. We know that no matter how much a nation may desire to hold itself aloof and to keep apart from the struggle it cannot escape war's terrible effects.

"An appreciation of even these two things should influence nations to leave nothing undone that would help in even the slightest degree to lessen the possibility of international strife.

"We know that there is no glory in war, either in its methods or in its results, and that its only glory is the glory of a sacrifice for the ideals which are involved."

When views like that are put before the minds of great bodies of men by such as General Currie there is a hope that reason will prevail over unreason, and that we may exorcise that infernal

[235]

spectre of another world war which lurks in our bad dreams.

CLASS WARFARE

But we must first kill the idea of force and violence between classes as well as nations. There will be no world peace if those who preach the virtue of international brotherhood are at the same time organising a class warfare in a spirit of intolerance that is abominable. In many countries of the world —and the most civilised—at this present date, the nations are being divided by a passionate opposition between ideas roughly labelled as Capital and Labour, Liberty and Tyranny, Bolshevism and Fascism. In England the Left Wing of the Labour Party is using wild and whirling words which are a disgrace to civilised men and women. They are advocating "an orgy of blood" to overthrow the capitalist system and establish equality of labour in all countries. At a meeting in the Memorial Hall, London, last August, the Communists put forward a programme of violence which was an outrageous defiance of the moderate counsels of Ramsay MacDonald and his colleagues, and proposed a charter of labour "rights," including a thirty-hour working week, which would bring Great Britain to the depths of ruin in a very short time. On the other side the English "Die-hards" are organising a secret society of Fascisti on the Italian lines, for the defence of property, national discipline, and resistance to all liberal ideas. Intolerance, the spirit of violence, are at work among the extremists on both sides, both narrow-minded and ignorant, both asking for trouble, both believing in force rather than in argument, arbitration, and law. In England, by the grace of God and long tradition, there is between these two extremes a great body of middle class, moderate, reasonable, and steady opinion which is the safeguard of the nation against all violent revolution. The aristocracy as a whole is liberal, kindly and self-sacrificing, and by no means disposed to play into the hands of its own extremists represented by the Duke of Northumberland and that remarkable lady, Mrs. Nesta Webster. The Labour Party as long as it is led by its present chiefs is contemptuous of Mr. Tom Mann and his loud-throated "comrades." Nevertheless the devil of intolerance is making disciples on both sides.

Not only in England. There are many little

Mussolinis about the world who are in favour of tyranny under the name of discipline and prefer hammering their political opponents in a physical way rather than converting them by arguments and beating them at the polls. There are many little Lenins skulking about factory yards or drawing good salaries as labour agitators who have equal scorn for the old traditions of Parliamentary Government and the Common Law of the land, and advocate short cuts to the equality of men by "the Dictatorship of the Proletariat"—which allows no equality to those who disagree with their point of view—and by violent assault upon the lives and property of the middle classes.

THE CHALLENGE OF INTOLERANCE

The old liberal principles of free speech, religious liberty, racial equality before the law and obedience to the law itself, until it is altered by the will of the majority, is being attacked from both wings on the Left and Right. The Swastika, or "Hackenkreuz," societies in Germany and Austria, becoming very powerful and aggressive, have declared war against the Jews, and vengeance against

France. In Hungary the persecution of Jews is a passionate article of faith among those who support the present dictatorship. In the United States of America the Ku Klux Klan defies the very spirit of liberty and law which inspired the American constitution and preaches Intolerance as its creed—intolerance of Jews, intolerance of the Negro Race, intolerance of Catholics, intolerance of political labour. It is a secret society which seems to me in violent conflict with all the idealism stirring in the soul of America. If it is not checked or killed by public opinion it will certainly lead to social conflict in the United States of very grave consequences. The argument of the Ku Klux Klansmen that they stand for purity in politics, the old traditions of American character menaced by the tyranny and corruption of Irish politicians, Jewish financiers and Labour revolutionaries, seems to me no defence of their methods or their principles. It is not by defiance of the law that they will exact obedience to the law. It is not by setting up a secret government that they will destroy Tammany which is also a secret government. It is not by spreading a propaganda of hate against the Jewish race—which has been greatly loyal to American ideals and

by its genius has brought great wealth in art, music
and literature as well as in dollars to the United
States—that the gospel of Christianity will be more
faithfully observed. It is not by burning Catholic
Churches that Christ will be served. It is not by
lynch law against negroes or any other class of
American citizens that the United States is going to
give a spiritual lead to the world or improve its own
state of civilisation. All that is a hark-back to
barbarity and not a stride forward to a more civilised world. It is the revival of cruelty which we
want to slay with other qualities of the beast in us.
It is the spirit of "Prussianism" against which we
were supposed to be fighting in the great war.

It is true of course that tolerance cannot be
carried to extreme limits. One cannot tolerate ob-
scenity, incitements to murder, or to "orgies of
blood" in the cause of "liberty," or revolutionary
attacks upon the ordinary rights of citizenship and
the common law of the land. There comes a point
when tolerance must become intolerance unless it
makes an abject surrender to the forces of evil and
anarchy. That is the argument of those who justify
Mussolini and his Fascisti, the Ku Klux Klan, the
Swastika societies in Germany, and the "Die-hards"

in England. It is a sound argument when that point of conscience is reached. But the danger of intolerance is far greater than that of tolerance, and it is apt to encourage and inflame the very evils which it is opposing. Free speech is a great safety valve for overheated air as the English people have found through centuries of history, and are finding now. Revolution is most dangerous when it is driven underground by autocracy and tyranny. Above all, religious and racial equality before the law is the foundation of all civilised states. Without that a state is not only uncivilised but its form of government is doomed to destruction, as history has shewn a thousand times.

THE SACRED REMEMBRANCE

Ten years after the beginning of the World War, fought on our side with a high appeal to such great words as "Liberty," "Justice," "a world made safe for democracy" and "the overthrow of militarism," one is dismayed to find the beginning of a class warfare with appeals to force, and denials of liberty and justice, on both sides. Surely the one sacred remembrance worth keeping, the only glory that belonged to that war, is the spiritual emotion which for a time exalted our common clay above self-interest, above the fear of death itself, and united all classes in the nation in a comradeship of sacrifice and service. It was so in Germany as well as in England, in the United States as well as in France. Each side believed itself to be in the right, prayed God for aid with no sense of blasphemy.

Never before in history, at least in France, England and the United States, was there such a "sacred union" of all ranks and classes under the first impulse of that immense emotion for a single purpose. All political differences were blotted out, all prerogatives of caste and wealth, all hatreds between groups of men, all intolerance, were waived. In those days, as I have written, the society women went down on their knees to scrub floors for the wounded, or served as drudges in wayside canteens. In those days, ten years ago, the young aristocrat marvelled at the splendour of his men—"nothing was too good for them." In those days before the time of disillusion the men were uplifted by the love of the nation that went out to them. There was no spirit of class warfare, no Bolshevism, no hatred of "Labour." The dirtiest soldier in the trenches, covered with mud and blood, was our national hero. Our soul did homage to him. And between the wounded soldier, lying in his shell-hole beside his wounded officer, and that officer there was no hostility, no gulf of class. They were crucified together on the same cross. They were comrades in agony and death.

It was for war. The service which united all classes was the slaughter of men on the other side of the line drawn across the map of the world, or the provision of means of slaughter. That intense impulse of devotion, sacrifice and duty which in its first manifestations had something divine in its carelessness of self—in all countries—was in its effects destructive of the best human life in the world. Is it too much for humanity to get that same impulse for the cause of peace, to get back to that comradeship and co-operation within those nations for other purposes than that of war, to rise above self-interest for the commonwealth of civilisation?

It is very difficult, almost impossible, I think, without tremendous leadership which we cannot yet perceive. War is a shock which thrills every soul by its terrific portent. Peace is a state in which the smaller interests of life seem more important than

[243]

great issues. War provides the people with a single dominating purpose, inspired by passion. Peace has no definite goal to capture or defend, and human intelligence is divided by a million views in its gropings for the ideals of peace. It is only danger that rallies the human tribes in self-defence. In safety they scatter and are hostile to each other.

Well, the danger ahead is great enough, in my judgment, to provide the impulse again, and to re-create the passion which united classes and nations ten years ago. If we have that "next war" it is going to thrust us all into deep pits of ruin. If we have social warfare within the civilised nations we shall not emerge from it until tides of blood have flowed. If we have an unrestricted commercial war, a savage and ruthless competition between great powers out for world trade at all costs against each other, the other things will happen. The human tribes in the next phase of history, now approaching, must co-operate or perish.

There is no one cure for all these troubles, but they may be lessened, and their greatest perils averted surely by a spirit of reason against unreason, by tolerance against intolerance, by ideals of peace against ideals of force, by conciliation against conflict, by a change of heart in the individual as well as in the nation.

GOD OR THE DEVIL?

It comes back to that as it has always come back. Are we going to serve God or Devils? Is the Christian world going to crucify Christ again or obey His commands? There are many religions in the world, but all men have the same God in their hearts. Catholic, Protestant or Jew, Mohammedan, Hindu or Buddhist, the God that is revealed to them has the same attributes of mercy, justice, love, under whatever name they worship the Spirit. It is because men are disloyal to their God that the world is afflicted by so much unnecessary evil, by so many tragedies and tears.

The Christian peoples at least are dedicated to peace, by words that they cannot ignore without treachery to the spirit of their faith. There is no Christianity in hatred, none in class warfare, none in violence against our neighbour, none in envy of our neighbour's goods, none in denial of the labourer's hire, none without love and pity and self-sacrifice. It is only by re-dedicating ourselves to that spirit that we can hope to solve the problems that beset us on every side and exorcise the evil powers in the heart of humanity which are working for destruction.

Ten years after the World War civilisation is still unsafe. Ten years after the great sacrifice of youth peace is not assured for the babes who are now in their cradles. But, ten years after, there is the beginning, at last, of a world opinion rising up against the war makers, eager for some new form of international law, determined to prevent another massacre of young manhood by the science and machinery of destruction, aware of the evil forces that are working for new conflict. The tides of hate are on the ebb in many countries. The spirit of peace is spreading, if slowly. It is the hope ahead.

Ten years after let us remember the splendour and the spirit of the youth that died for ideals not yet fulfilled.

THE END